YOLELE!
RECIPES FROM
THE HEART
OF SENEGAL

LAKE
ISLE
PRESS

YOLELE!

RECIPES FROM THE HEART OF SENEGAL

BY PIERRE THIAM

PHOTOGRAPHY BY ADAM BARTOS

Published by:
Lake Isle Press, Inc.
16 West 32nd Street, Suite 10-B
New York, NY 10001
(212) 273-0796
E-mail: lakeisle@earthlink.net

Distributed to the trade by:
National Book Network, Inc.
4501 Forbes Boulevard, Suite 200
Lanham, MD 20706
1 (800) 462-6420
www.nbnbooks.com

Library of Congress Control Number:
2008929056
ISBN-13: 978-1-891105-38-8

Book and cover design:
Luke Hayman, Pentagram

Editors: Pimpila Thanaporn
Katherine Trimble

Credits: The publisher acknowledges the
kind cooperation of the Kiln Design Studio
of Brooklyn, NY (www.kilnenamel.com) for
the use of their fine enamelware.

This book is available at special sales
discounts for bulk purchases as premiums
or special editions, including customized
covers. For more information, contact the
publisher at (212) 273-0796 or by e-mail,
lakeisle@earthlink.net

First edition
Printed in the United States of America

10 9 8 7 6 5 4 3 2 1

To Umaimah, Sitoë, Elijah, Haroun, and to Maman

CONTENTS

Fish boulettes, white rice, and assorted vegetables

Aunt Marie preparing to roast stuffed fish

Mamma Douba Kande

INTRODUCTION

I n Senegal, cooking is a celebration, a happy recognition of our ages-old patrimony and all the influences that have informed it from the time of the Arab incursions through colonization and on to the present, when we can boast influences from Vietnam to the Americas. It's a celebration, too, of how we have gloriously melded the old with the new, the native with the global, and arrived at what is arguably the most sophisticated cuisine in all of Africa.

Our expression, *Yolélé!*, reminds me very much of the Louisiana Creole, *Laissez les bon temps rouler!* ("Let the good times roll"). This reflects the similarities, practical and cultural, between our cultures, including the French trappings that ice the cake. When I came to this country and got to know America's Creole history and cuisine, it felt comfortingly familiar, and then I discovered how many dishes were directly related to the western shores of Africa.

Senegal, with a long Atlantic coastline and a climate that varies from arid to semi-tropical, is rich in the resources of land and sea. Since the Senegalese insist on only the freshest ingredients, nearly all our produce is grown and sold locally. So the habit of buying fresh daily has, fortunately, withstood the influence of the Western practice of one-stop weekly shopping. A refreshing example of this strong tradition is the early morning haggling over just-caught fish, a vibrant scene enacted daily on the beaches of our many coastal towns. The various cultures whose people have come to Senegal as traders and colonizers have also had a great influence on our cuisine. In fact, we have a word heard all over Senegal, *teranga*, that is used to welcome people to our homes and our table. It is a key to how we've assimilated various cultures throughout the centuries.

I grew up in a multicultural milieu. I was raised in Dakar, the cosmopolitan capital of Senegal. My neighborhood was mixed, African and European. I spent summers and holidays in rural Casamance, my family's base in the south of the country. Much of Casamance lies on the sea, and while it is steeped in the traditions of a number of African

peoples, the region also was imprinted by the former colonial presence of Portugal. The result is a unique, Creole culture. In fact the word *Casamance* is a sonorous synthesis of the Portuguese *casa*, or house, with the Mandinka, *mansa* or king—or, "house of the king." (The Mandinka are a large ethnic group inhabiting large areas of Mali, Guinea Bissau, Gambia, and southern Senegal). Ziguinchor, Casamance's capital, combines two Portuguese words given decidedly Mandinka pronunciations, *chegar*, "to arrive," and *chorar*, "to cry." Legend has it that when the Portuguese arrived in Ziguinchor, a funeral was in progress, and they came upon many people in tears. Thus we became known as "the crying town of others' arrival."

It was in the Creole milieu of Casamance where I became most excited about food. My parents' ancestors came from disparate parts of the country, with Casamance their common ground. Creole became their common language. In fact, we spoke Portuguese Creole at home more than Wolof[1] (Senegal's lingua franca) or French.

The time I spent with Tonton Jean, my uncle from Vietnam, was also very influential. He was the first man I'd ever seen in the kitchen; he worked magic with exotic and local flavors, and cultivated a little miracle garden of Senegalese and Vietnamese delights. Also inspiring were the special occasions—baby-naming days, weddings, first communions—when my aunts from all over the country would arrive to work with my mother, preparing a medley of traditional dishes. Because I was raised in a part-Christian and part-Muslim extended family, there was hardly enough time after one feast was over before we'd have to get ready for another one. I got to enjoy Muslim specialties such as roast lamb for *Tabaski*,[2] and Christian delicacies like pork *yassa* with onions and lime, the next.

Senegalese traditions are given life through the *griots*, men and women who transmit our history through the spoken and sung word. They often sing for their suppers, praising the hands of noted cooks in their incantations as a way of ensuring delicious and plentiful food in their bowls. Our cuisine has been passed down through oral tradition, too. For hundreds of years, women taught their daughters and nieces and neighbors their culinary secrets, and it is only recently that we've felt the need to make written records of our recipes.

Now that we've embraced the written word and foreign influences, our food breathes differently, even more intriguingly, than before. These new culinary currents have washed over me, gotten caught in

1. Wolof is the main language in Senegal. Most people speak it fluently. The Wolof people represent a majority among the seven ethnic groups that coexist there.

2. This holiday is a Muslim celebration of Abraham's biblical story. Each faithful family offers a lamb in sacrifice to Allah. When the lamb is slaughtered, the meat is divided into three portions: One for the family, one for the Christian neighbors and friends, and one for the needy. In turn, Christians offer *ngalakh*, a millet and peanut delicacy, to their Muslim friends on Good Friday. The ritual of sharing food between Muslims and Christians contributes to making Senegal a particularly tolerant country.

Aunt Marie stirs her lamb stew

3. *P'tit Poucet* translates to "little thumb." My mother was a petite woman and her friends nicknamed her after the hero of the French tale *Le P'tit Poucet*.

my woolly hair and under my voluminous *bubu*, influencing my own approach to cuisine.

My mother, Marie Madeleine, affectionately called P'tit Poucet,[3] loved to cook. I remember the many feasts she would prepare with her sisters and cousins at our home in Dakar or in the ancestral compound in Casamance. In Dakar, Maman often experimented with European dishes, and I spent many hours pouring over her *Larousse Gastronomique* collection while my friends were making a racket out in the street playing soccer and taunting the girls.

It was the combined artistry of my tireless, ever-exploring mother and Tonton Jean that inspired me to cook. However, cultural restraints forbade me from considering cooking as a profession when I was still home. Men in Senegal just don't cook.

In the States, however, a surprisingly large number of Senegalese cook professionally. Many are women who make ends meet by running small, homey eateries tucked into apartments in the tenements where they live. These serve as lunchtime pit stops for West African cabbies and merchants. Most Senegalese men who cook here in the States had experiences like mine: They learned at home by observing the women of their households. In this country, they tend to work in kitchens that turn out anything but Senegalese food. Little of our cuisine is known outside our own communities. As a result, I feel I've been pioneering a cuisine that is both familiar and exotic, offering fare that is both down-home and elegant.

The recipes in this book reflect my personal odyssey, my travels through West Africa, Europe, and finally here, where, from my New York address, I've seen the world. They showcase the repertoire of the contemporary Senegalese home cook, representing a mix of the age-old (*thiebou jen*, spicy stuffed fish with vegetables and rice), and the more modern (Vietnamese-influenced shrimp and melon salad).

The chapter on recipes carried over from Africa to the New World is one of continuing discovery for me and speaks to the creolization that has both defined and intrigued me since childhood. Included, for example, is our *accara*, black-eyed pea fritters, which became *acaraje* in Brazil; and *soupou kandja*, reborn in New Orleans as shrimp gumbo. These recipes represent the Middle Passage, the memories of a whole culture, which are a part of my personal journey, while for the reader they bridge new African recipes and the old glories of the American table. In working on this chapter, I especially thought of people of African descent—African-Americans, Afro-Caribbeans, or Afro-Latinos—who would find distant familiarities in the dishes that didn't travel and a sense of home in those that did.

This book has been stirring within me for many years. It is a major focus of my yearly trips home, revisiting old food experiences, seeking out what is new, taking notes to record my impressions. I've compiled these recipes with home cooks in mind, those with curiosity not only for the exotic but also for flavors that offer something new yet feel familiar.

APPETIZERS
AND STREET FOOD

Green Mango Salad (Niambaan)

Outside my bedroom window in Senegal we had a mango tree so huge, its branches hung over our neighbor's courtyard. Sometimes, I couldn't wait for the fruit to ripen and would gather them for this dish. *Niambaan* can refer to a variety of sour fruits seasoned with salt and chile pepper, but the most commonly used are green mangoes or tamarind. Here is a variation of a similar salad that hails from Vietnam.

2 garlic cloves, minced

1/2 teaspoon salt

2 teaspoons sugar

2 tablespoons rice wine vinegar or lime juice

1 habanero pepper, seeded and thinly sliced

2 or 3 unripe green mangoes, peeled and coarsely shredded

1 carrot, peeled and coarsely grated

1 cup chopped cilantro

SERVES 4

1. Combine the garlic, salt, sugar, and rice wine vinegar or lime juice, stir to blend. Set aside.

2. In a large bowl, combine the habanero, shredded mango, carrot, and cilantro. Add the dressing and toss well.

Salad Niokolo

The inspiration for this salad comes from chef Ndecky at the *Ecole Hôtelière* in Dakar. It is named after a wildlife reservation in the southeast, near Guinea and Mali.

3 quarts court bouillon (see recipe page 46)

2 pounds shrimp (U/10), cleaned and deveined, tails attached

1 teaspoon salt

1/2 teaspoon ground white pepper

Juice of 1 lemon

1 garlic clove, minced

1/2 cup extra-virgin olive oil

1 unripe green papaya, peeled and grated

1/2 cup shredded unsweetened coconut

10 cherry tomatoes

SERVES 4

1. In a medium pot, bring the court bouillon to a boil. Briskly blanch the shrimp until just cooked, about 1 minute. Remove to an ice bath to prevent further cooking. Reserve.

2. Make the vinaigrette: With a whisk, dissolve the salt and pepper in the lemon juice. Add the minced garlic. Still whisking, slowly pour the extra-virgin olive oil into the lemon juice mixture to create an emulsion.

3. In a small bowl, combine grated green papaya and shredded coconut. Drizzle a few tablespoons of vinaigrette over it and toss.

4. To serve, mound the coconut-papaya salad in the center of a plate and surround with the shrimp, tail ends pointing towards the edge of the plate. Garnish with cherry tomatoes and drizzle more dressing over the shrimp.

In the village of Elinkine with my aunts and cousins

Tempra

A classic from the shores of Guinea Bissau to the Casamance river, *tempra* is somewhat reminiscent of a Peruvian ceviche, the major difference being that here we grill the shrimp or oysters before marinating them in the lemon mixture. *Tempra* goes well with steamed white rice.

2 pounds prawns, halved lengthwise

1/4 cup peanut oil, plus 2 tablespoons

Salt and freshly ground black pepper

1 red onion, finely julienned

2 firm ripe tomatoes, chopped

1/2 cup fresh lemon juice

1 habanero pepper, finely chopped

SERVES 4

1. Preheat a grill pan or outdoor grill over high heat. Rub the prawns with about 2 tablespoons oil, and the salt and pepper. Grill until tender and just cooked through.

2. Place the onions and tomatoes in a salad bowl along with remaining 1/4 cup peanut oil, the lemon juice, salt, pepper, and habanero. Add the grilled shrimp and combine. Allow to sit for at least 30 minutes before serving. Serve at room temperature.

Spicy Grilled Kebabs (Dibi Hausa)

Come summer, while vacationing at my grandparents' home in Casamance, I'd always look forward to feasting on Seyni's *dibi hausa*. This tall, skinny, middle-aged man from Niger made the best *dibi hausa* in the world—his wooden shack was always crowded. He had a long, narrow wooden bench inside the hut that was always lined with hungry patrons. I remember the inviting glow from the fire that penetrated through the cracks between the worn boards and the rich, woodsy aroma that wafted out in clouds of cooking smoke. Every day Seyni would grill hundreds of these tender lamb skewers coated with a spice mix known as *tankora* and served with spicy, thinly-sliced raw onions on top. Here I use beef.

This popular snack originates in Hausa land, located in northern Nigeria and southeastern Niger, today's northern reaches of the domain of the nomadic Hausa people who travel throughout West Africa in search of pastureland for their cattle.

1 pound round steak, cut into strips about 1 1/2 inches wide by 2 inches long and 3/8 inch thick

1/4 teaspoon finely grated fresh ginger

1/2 teaspoon minced garlic

2 1/2 tablespoons finely grated onion

1 tablespoon tomato paste

1 chicken bouillon cube, crumbled (optional)

1 tablespoon peanut oil

1/2 teaspoon salt

1/2 teaspoon cayenne pepper

1 teaspoon white pepper

1 cup *tankora* powder (recipe follows)

8 (6-inch) skewers (if using wooden skewers, soak them in water for an hour to prevent them from burning on the grill)

SERVES 4 TO 6

1. Preheat a grill pan or outdoor grill over high heat, or start the broiler. In a bowl, combine the meat, ginger, garlic, onion, tomato paste, and bouillon cube, if using. Add the oil, salt, and cayenne and white peppers and stir well to blend. Allow to marinate 10 to 15 minutes.

2. Thread a few slices of meat onto each skewer. Pour the *tankora* powder onto a plate and roll each skewer in it, evenly coating all sides. Shake off the excess powder. With a pastry brush, brush about 1 teaspoon marinade over each skewer. Place the skewers over grill and cook 5 minutes on each side. Keep brushing with marinade while grilling to prevent them from drying out. Alternatively, the kebabs can be broiled in the oven a few inches from the heat.

Tankora Powder
(Hausa Spice Mix)

1 cup roasted unsalted peanuts,
   crushed to a fine powder

1/2 teaspoon ground cayenne pepper

1 teaspoon ground ginger

1 teaspoon salt

1 teaspoon freshly ground white pepper

MAKES ABOUT 1 CUP

1. Combine all the ingredients. Keep in an airtight jar for up to 2 months.

Grilled Sea Urchin

One of our favorite activities as kids was to find sea urchins. They would hide under rocks by the shore, and all we had to do was to dive into the water to access their hideaways. This activity wasn't without its risks, though. With no goggles and only our bare hands, we had to grab these curious creatures delicately, being careful not to get pricked by their spiny armor. That accomplished, we would build a fire from dead wood and simply grill our harvest. The aroma first, and then the taste of the delicious grilled sea urchin roe was our well-won reward. Whoever first said, "the simpler the better," must have been a sea urchin hunter on a beach in Dakar.

12 sea urchins

Juice of 1 lemon

SERVES 4 TO 6

1. Preheat a broiler, grill pan, or outdoor grill over high heat. Cook sea urchins 10 to 15 minutes. The spines will fall off once cooked. Crack shell and extract roe. Squeeze lemon juice over the meat and enjoy as is, with the extracted roe on the side.

Fish and Corn Fritters (Beignets Mboqu Jenn)

2 to 3 fillets firm-fleshed fish,
    such as carp, tilapia, or snapper
    (1 pound total)

2 quarts court bouillon (see recipe
    page 46)

2 cups cornmeal

2 quarts water

1/2 cup all-purpose flour

1 teaspoon baking soda

2 tablespoons vegetable oil,
    plus 1 quart for frying

1/2 onion, finely chopped

3 scallions, finely chopped

4 garlic cloves, finely chopped

2 green bell peppers, seeded and
    finely chopped

1 habanero pepper, finely chopped

1 pinch salt

1 pinch freshly ground black pepper

2 large eggs, lightly beaten

1 bunch curly parsley, finely chopped

MAKES 30 BEIGNETS

1. In a medium saucepan over medium-high heat, cook the fish fillets in court bouillon until flaky to the touch, about 8 to 10 minutes. Strain, reserving the bouillon and let the fish cool while you keep the bouillon hot.

2. In a large bowl, combine the cornmeal and 2 quarts water to obtain a runny batter.

3. Add the cornmeal mixture to 1 quart reserved hot court bouillon. Simmer, stirring with a wooden spoon, about 10 minutes. Remove from heat. Let cool until tepid. Add the flour and baking soda, stirring until dissolved.

4. Flake the cooked fish with a fork and combine with the cornmeal mixture.

5. In a pan over medium heat, add 2 tablespoons vegetable oil and sauté the onions, scallions, garlic, green pepper, habanero, salt, and black pepper until softened. Add to the cornmeal mixture. Add the eggs and parsley and mix together. With your hands, shape mixture into ovals (about 2 tablespoon each).

6. Heat remaining oil in a large pan to 365°F. Fry fritters until golden brown and serve hot with *kaani* sauce (see recipe page 115).

Millet-Beef Croquettes (Karakoro)

2 cups water, plus 1/4 cup for diluting flour

1/2 pound ground beef

1/2 cup finely chopped onion

3 garlic cloves, finely chopped

Salt and freshly ground black pepper

1 cup millet flour

1 teaspoon baking soda

2 tablespoons vegetable oil, plus more for deep-frying

2 large eggs

SERVES 8

1. Bring 2 cups water to a boil in a medium saucepan. Add the ground beef, onion, and garlic. Season with salt and pepper and cook about 5 minutes over high heat.

2. In a small bowl, combine the millet flour and baking soda in 1/4 cup water, stirring until a thick batter forms. Add to the pot and stir until the mixture thickens. Turn off the heat and let cool completely.

3. In a small bowl, briefly whisk 2 tablespoons oil into the eggs and fold into the meat mixture. Shape the mixture into walnut-size balls.

4. Heat 2 inches oil in a deep skillet until it reaches 365°F. Deep-fry the croquettes until lightly golden, about 2 to 3 minutes. Serve hot with *kaani* sauce (see recipe page 115).

Pastels

Pastels—the name is derived from the Spanish word for most anything under a pastry crust—are the quintessential street food throughout Senegal. Women in voluminous, brightly colored *bubus* set up shop outside markets and soccer stadiums and on street corners, and plant themselves behind rickety wooden tables, their faces sweaty and aglow, a charcoal brazier burning at their side. They sell pastels to shoppers, school kids, and strollers throughout the day and into the night, dropping them, piping hot, into cones rolled from brown construction paper; the pastels are then topped off by the spicy *kaani* sauce, and after but a few CFA (the Senegalese currency) are exchanged, everyone is quite content.

4 onions, minced

2 garlic cloves, minced

2 tablespoons vegetable oil, plus more for frying

1 habanero pepper, seeded and chopped

2 pounds mackerel or mullet fillets, finely chopped

2 tablespoons chopped cilantro

Salt and freshly ground black pepper

1 package empanada dough (such as Goya brand, about 10 disks total)

***Kaani* sauce (see recipe page 115)**

MAKES ABOUT 20 PASTELS

1. In a pan over medium heat, sauté the onions and garlic in 2 tablespoons oil until soft but not brown, about 5 minutes. Remove and place them in a mixing bowl along with the habanero.

2. Bring a medium saucepan filled halfway with water to a simmer. Insert the fish and poach until cooked through, 7 to 10 minutes, depending on its thickness. Remove fish from water.

3. With a fork, flake the cooked fish and add to the onion-habanero mixture along with the chopped cilantro. Season with salt and pepper, stir, and set aside.

4. Cut the empanada discs in half and put 1 tablespoon fish mixture in the middle of each half. Fold the dough over the mixture, crimping the edges with a fork to close tightly.

5. Fill a large pan with vegetable oil about 2 inches deep; place over medium-high heat. When oil reaches 365°F, fry the *pastels* in batches until nicely golden, without crowding the pan. Serve hot with *kaani* sauce in brown paper cones, or plated over lettuce leaves.

Peppe' Soup

This soup must be eaten spicy hot. From Nigeria to Senegal it is known as the partygoer's breakfast. Peppe' soup gets you back on your feet after a late night of drinking. Of course, one does not need to drink to appreciate this toe-curling, delicious fish soup.

2 whole fish, such as grouper, snapper, or sea bass, cut into pieces, heads reserved (4 pounds total)

1 yuca (about 1/2 pound), peeled, cored, and cubed

4 onions, chopped

1 garlic clove, crushed

1 habanero pepper

1 bay leaf

2 quarts water

Salt

Juice of 4 limes, or to taste

SERVES 6

1. Place the fish in a large pot with the yuca, onions, garlic, habanero, bay leaf, and water. Over medium heat, bring the liquid to a simmer. Cook until the yuca is tender, about 30 minutes. Turn off the heat and let cool until cool enough to handle.

2. Using a slotted spoon, remove the fish and set it on a platter. Remove the flesh from the bones with your fingers and reserve, discarding the bones and bay leaf.

3. Place the soup, except the reserved fish, in the bowl of a food processor. Add salt and process until velvety. Add the lime juice, to taste. Adjust the seasoning. Add the reserved fish and serve hot.

Fried Sweet Plantains (Aloco)

This popular street food from the Côte d'Ivoire is sold in open-air markets called *alocodromes*, where the specialty is fried plantain, any style. Come dusk, the *alocodromes* become a trendy spot where the hip Abidjan youth come for a snack. They gather around women using battered aluminum cooking pots, loads of ripe plantains laying on the ground at their feet. One hand stirs the gently frying *aloco*, the other wraps the treat in a piece of paper and counts the money.

1 quart palm or peanut oil, for frying

5 very ripe (to the point of blackness) plantains, peeled and cut on the diagonal into 1/2-inch rounds

***Kaani* sauce (see recipe page 115)**

SERVES 4

1. Heat the oil in a pot over medium heat until it reaches 365°F. Add plantain slices in batches and cook, turning occasionally, until well browned, about 5 minutes.

2. Remove plantains with a slotted spoon and drain on paper towels. Serve immediately with *kaani* sauce.

Shrimp and Sweet Potato Fritters

This is the Vietnamese answer to the *beignets de crevettes* from Saint-Louis, an old colonial town in the north of Senegal, famous for its exquisite cuisine and its charming women.

1 1/2 pounds medium shrimp, shelled and deveined

1 large sweet potato

1 teaspoon fish sauce (see Glossary)

2 scallions, finely sliced into ringlets

1 tablespoon freshly ground black pepper

1/4 cup all-purpose flour

1 teaspoon baking powder

1 large egg, lightly beaten

Peanut or vegetable oil, for frying

MAKES 8 TO 10 FRITTERS

1. Roughly chop the shrimp.

2. Shred the sweet potato using a box grater, processor, or mandoline.

3. In a large bowl, combine the sweet potatoes, shrimp, fish sauce, scallions, pepper, flour, baking powder, and egg and mix well with your hands or a spoon. Shape the batter into patties, using about 2 tablespoons batter per patty.

4. Fill a deep pan about 2 inches deep with oil and heat to 365°F. Gently fry the shrimp fritters until crisp and golden. Set on paper towels to drain as they are cooked. Serve hot with Vietnamese dipping sauce (*nuoc cham*; see recipe page 44).

Yucassoise

My inspiration for this cold summer soup is clearly the classic French vichyssoise, which I discovered in my mother's *Larousse Gastronomique*. As a child, I was intrigued by the idea of a cold soup. What's most satisfying about this variation is how the musty, starchy flavor of the yuca coaxes out the nuttiness of the familiar potato. Yuca was brought to the New World from Africa by the slaves and has become a staple in the Caribbean (where it's often called cassava) and Brazil (where it's known as mandioca).

4 leeks

2 tablespoons peanut oil

2 yuca, peeled and coarsely chopped

2 Idaho potatoes, peeled and coarsely chopped

2 onions, julienned

2 quarts chicken or vegetable stock

Salt

Freshly ground white pepper

1 quart milk (or chicken or vegetable stock)

SERVES 6

1. Cut 3 of the leeks in half lengthwise. Wash them thoroughly, running cold water in between the leaves to remove the sand. Coarsely chop them. Julienne the fourth leek and wash in cold water. Set aside for the garnish.

2. In a soup pot, heat the oil over medium heat; add the chopped leeks, yuca, potatoes, and onions. Cook slowly, covered, until onions are soft but not brown, stirring regularly, about 10 minutes.

3. Add the stock, increase the heat, and bring to a boil. Reduce the heat and simmer until all the ingredients are tender, about 25 minutes.

4. Season with salt and white pepper; add the milk if using, or the last quart of stock. Stir.

5. Puree the soup in a blender or food processor. Chill for several hours until quite cold. Alternatively, skip the pureeing and leave the soup chunky.

6. Blanch the reserved julienned leek, if using, in boiling water for 1 minute. Drain blanched leeks and let dry on a paper towel. Fry in hot oil until crispy and then drain. Top soup with fried leeks.

Coconut Chicken and Plantains en Papillote

2 chicken breasts (about 1 pound), very thinly sliced

Juice and grated zest of 1 lime

1 cup coconut milk

1 jalapeño pepper, seeded and very thinly sliced

1 pinch ground nutmeg

Salt

2 tablespoons unsweetened grated coconut

2 ripe plantains

1 very large banana leaf, cut into eight 6- to 8-inch squares

SERVES 4

1. Preheat the oven to 425°F. Place the sliced chicken in a large bowl and cover with lime juice. Let sit a few minutes then add the lime zest, coconut milk, jalapeño, nutmeg, salt, and grated coconut.

2. Peel and thinly slice the plantains. Rinse and pat dry the banana leaf squares. On the center of each square, set 2 or 3 plantain slices and 2 or 3 chicken slices, strained of the marinade. Close the leaf, folding the ends over. Secure with toothpicks or tie with kitchen twine. Continue the assembly until all the chicken is folded *en papillote*.

3. Place packets on a sheet pan and roast for about 20 minutes, testing once for doneness by opening one packet. Serve hot.

Palm fruit

Herbed Kefta

1 1/2 pounds ground beef or lamb, or a mixture of both

1 small onion, grated

1/3 cup finely chopped parsley

1 pinch chopped cilantro

4 large pinches freshly chopped mint

2 pinches fresh marjoram, or 1 large pinch dried

Salt and freshly ground black pepper

1/2 teaspoon ground cumin

1/2 teaspoon *ras el hanout* (see Glossary)

12 (6-inch) skewers (if you are using wooden skewers, soak them in water for an hour to prevent them from burning on the grill)

Roasted pepper salad (see recipe page 101)

Crispy toasted pita

SERVES 4

1. Combine the ground meat, onion, parsley, cilantro, mint, marjoram, salt, pepper, cumin, and *ras el hanout* in a large bowl and knead well until incorporated. Let sit at least 1 hour in the refrigerator.

2. Preheat a grill pan or outdoor grill over high heat. With wet hands, form the meat mixture into 24 sausage shapes, packing 2 around each skewer.

3. Grill rapidly on both sides. Serve hot at once with roasted pepper salad and crispy toasted pita.

Green Plantain Chips

4 large green plantains

Vegetable oil, for deep-frying

Salt

SERVES 4

1. Peel the plantain by cutting off the ends, then with a sharp knife, make a cut just through the skin along length of the plantain. Peel off the skin. Slice the peeled plantain into thin rounds or ovals or with a vegetable peeler cut horizontally along the plantain to make long thin slices.

2. Pour about 2 inches oil into a large saucepan. Heat the oil over medium-high heat to about 365°F. Drop the slices into the oil one by one, leaving room between the slices. Let them fry for a minute before lifting gently with a slotted metal spatula or fork. Remove when golden brown and drain on paper towels. Salt while the chips are still warm. The chips can be stored in an airtight container for up to 2 weeks.

Vegetarian Spring Rolls

If the Senegalese were to choose only one of "our" many Vietnamese dishes, *nems* would be the one. It's hard to imagine a party in Dakar without spring rolls. This is a vegetarian version.

1/2 cup dried tree-ear mushrooms

1 (2-ounce) package cellophane noodles, available in Asian markets

1 head cabbage, finely julienned

1 carrot, peeled and shredded

1 tablespoon fish sauce (see Glossary)

1 teaspoon salt

1 teaspoon freshly ground black pepper

2 garlic cloves, minced

1/2 cup chopped chives

2 tablespoons water

1 (1-pound) package of 8-inch round sheets of rice paper or wheat paper, available in Asian markets

Peanut oil, for deep-frying

3 heads iceberg, Boston, or Bibb lettuce, the large, unblemished leaves washed and reserved

1 1/2 cups loosely packed Thai basil, available in Asian markets (or use regular basil)

1 cup loosely packed fresh mint

2 cucumbers, peeled, seeded, and very thinly sliced

6 to 8 red chile peppers, sliced into thin rounds

Vietnamese Dipping Sauce (recipe follows)

MAKES 25 TO 30 SPRING ROLLS

1. Place the mushrooms and cellophane noodles in separate heatproof bowls. Cover with boiling water and let each ingredient soak for 15 minutes.

2. Meanwhile, in a large bowl, combine the cabbage, carrot, fish sauce, salt, black pepper, garlic, and chopped chives. Drain the mushrooms, chop, and add to the cabbage mix. Drain the cellophane noodles and roughly chop. Add the noodles to the cabbage and mix with your hands.

3. Taking one sheet at a time, brush each side of the rice paper liberally with water and set aside on a flat surface. Do not stack rice paper or they will stick together. Place 2 tablespoons filling in the center of a softened sheet. Fold the bottom flap over the filling, then roll the sheet and filling upward, toward the top, one time. Fold the sides in over the filling and continue to roll, pressing the edges to seal. Set each finished spring roll on a lightly oiled platter.

4. Heat a wok with about 4 inches of oil over medium heat to about 375°F. Arrange the lettuce leaves on one platter and the basil, mint, cucumber, and chile peppers on another. Place the dipping sauce in a small bowl.

5. Add the spring rolls to the hot oil, being careful not to overcrowd the wok. Fry about 5 minutes, turning from time to time. Remove and drain on paper towels. Repeat until all the spring rolls are cooked, but don't turn off the heat.

6. Turn up the heat slightly and fry the spring rolls in batches again for another minute to crisp them up. Remove and drain again thoroughly.

7. Set on a platter and serve immediately with the lettuce, garnishes, and the dipping sauce. To eat, take a lettuce leaf, put a spring roll in the center, top with any of the garnishes, roll up, dip in the sauce.

Vietnamese Dipping Sauce (Nuoc Cham)

This dipping sauce is great for spring rolls, grilled quail, or fish. Tonton Jean would garnish this sauce with thinly sliced raw carrot.

1/4 cup minced garlic

1/2 cup fish sauce (see Glossary)

1/3 cup fresh lime juice

1 tablespoon sugar

1 teaspoon chopped jalapeño pepper

5 tablespoons water

MAKES ABOUT 1 CUP

1. Mix together all the ingredients until the sugar is dissolved. Serve in small bowls for dipping.

Shrimp and Melon Salad

My uncle, Tonton Jean, was born and raised in Vietnam. His Senegalese father met his Vietnamese mother while serving in the French army, sent in to quell Indochina's struggle for independence. The whole family later moved to Senegal, and Tonton Jean became one of the significant influences contributing to my love for cuisine. Today, semi-retired, he grows redolent Vietnamese ingredients such as lemongrass, mint, and cilantro in his garden in Dakar.

All Senegalese have taken to Vietnamese food, thanks to the many families who have immigrated in much the same way as Tonton Jean's. What's more, Saveurs d'Asie, Vietnamese-owned, is the largest restaurant chain in all of Senegal—our McDonalds, but with exotic flavors. Kermel, an open-air market in which many of the providers are Vietnamese, is one of the most intriguing spots in all of Dakar, a feast of sights and flavors.

1 quart court bouillon (recipe follows)

1 pound small shrimp (size 16/20)

1 teaspoon shrimp paste (see Glossary)

2 tablespoons fish sauce (see Glossary)

2 teaspoons finely chopped ginger

2 tablespoons chopped fresh mint

2 stalks lemongrass

1 jalapeño pepper, chopped

1 cup fresh lime juice

1 small cantaloupe, peeled and diced

1/2 cup shelled roasted peanuts

SERVES 6

1. In a large saucepan, bring court bouillon to a boil. Add the shrimp, lower to a simmer, and poach 2 minutes. Cool, then peel, devein, and roughly chop the shrimp.

2. Prepare the dressing by blending the shrimp paste, fish sauce, ginger, mint, lemongrass, jalapeño, and lime juice in a blender or food processor.

3. To assemble, toss the melon, shrimp, and roasted peanuts with the dressing until well blended. Serve at room temperature.

Court Bouillon

1 carrot, thinly sliced

2 onions, thinly sliced

2 tablespoons peanut oil

4 cups water

1 cup dry white wine

1 teaspoon salt

6 white peppercorns

1 *bouquet garni* (bay leaf, 3 sprigs parsley, and a celery leaf tied together with string)

MAKES ABOUT 1 QUART

1. In a large saucepan over medium heat, saute carrot and onions in the oil without browning. Add the other ingredients and bring to a boil. Strain out solids and discard. Cool.

Chaf

To me, this is the ultimate beach snack. On most beaches in Senegal you will notice women dressed in colorful fabrics, selling these salty, crunchy peanuts freshly sifted from a wok full of hot sea sand.

1 quart water

1/2 cup salt

1 pound raw peanuts, shelled

2 pounds sea sand

MAKES ABOUT 3 CUPS

1. Fill a large mixing bowl with the water and add the salt. Soak the peanuts in the salted water for about 2 hours. Preheat the oven to 200°F. Drain nuts and spread on a large cookie sheet. Place in oven for about 15 minutes to dry nuts completely.

2. Meanwhile, fill a wok halfway up with sea sand. Sit the wok on a wok rack above a high flame until the sand is hot. Add the peanuts, stirring constantly until the peanuts are crunchy and their skins slip off easily, about 30 minutes. Away from the heat, sift the peanuts and sand through a colander. Remove the peanuts to a bowl and serve.

Avocado-Mango Salad

This salad is inspired by cherished times I had as a child in my grandparents' yard in Casamance, which is filled with avocado and mango trees. Both fruits, contrasting in aroma, flavor, intensity, and texture, have remained favorites through the years. This salad not only combines the velvety comfort of the avocado and the sweetly acidic flavor of the mango, but adds spark with the piquant chile.

1 tablespoon fresh lime juice

Salt and freshly ground black pepper

1/4 cup peanut oil

1 jalapeño pepper, stemmed and minced

1 cup parsley leaves, chopped

2 ripe mangoes

2 ripe avocados

1/4 cup chopped tomatoes

SERVES 4

1. Mix the lime juice with salt and pepper and whisk in the oil. Add the jalapeño and stir with a fork. Add the parsley and stir.

2. Peel and pit the mangoes, then slice them lengthwise about 1/8-inch thick. Place them in a bowl and pour half the dressing over them. Let marinate at room temperature for half an hour or in the refrigerator for 1 hour.

3. Fan the mango slices halfway around each of 4 serving plates. Just before serving, peel the avocados and cut into 1/8-inch-thick slices. Arrange them in a fan mirroring the mango arrangement and leaving a small well in the center of the plate. Reserving 2 tablespoons of the dressing, pour what remains over the avocado slices. Toss the chopped tomatoes with the remaining 2 tablespoons of dressing and place in the center of each serving plate.

Madame Amy Aris

Madame Rokhaya Diallo

Fonio & Smoked Tofu Stuffed Tomatoes (Tomates Farcies au Fonio et Tofu Fumé)

6 large tomatoes

1/2 cup fonio (see Glossary)

1 Kirby cucumber, peeled and finely diced

1/4 cup diced smoked tofu, available in health food stores

1 teaspoon fresh lime juice

1 teaspoon salt, plus more for tomatoes

1/2 cup olive oil

Basil, julienned, for garnish

SERVES 6

1. Cut 1 inch off the top of the tomatoes and keep the "hat." With a spoon, scrape out the seeds of the tomatoes and discard. Salt the inside of each tomato (just a pinch for each tomato) and set upside down on a rack for 30 minutes to drain their water.

2. Meanwhile, place the fonio in the top of a steamer basket lined with cheesecloth and steam until tender and fluffy, 20 minutes. Let cool.

3. In a bowl, fold cucumber and tofu into the cooked fonio. Place the lime juice in a bowl and whisk in 1 teaspoon salt; slowly add the olive oil, while whisking, to create an emulsion. Dress fonio mixture with this vinaigrette and stuff the tomatoes. Garnish with the basil and top with reserved tomato "hat."

Sesame Fonio

2 teaspoons peanut oil

1/2 cup black sesame seeds

3 cups water

Pinch salt

1 cup fonio (see Glossary)

MAKES 3 CUPS

1. Heat the oil in a skillet over medium heat. Add sesame seeds; stir and cook until fragrant.

2. Meanwhile, in a saucepan, bring the water and salt to a boil. Add fonio and sautéed sesame seeds. Return to a boil, reduce heat and simmer for about 7 more minutes until all water is absorbed. Stir to fluff. Can be eaten as a side dish with fish or chicken.

Grilling gambas at Jeanine Diop's

SEAFOOD

Crab St. Louis Style (Cotis Ndar)

The huge crabs caught in the mouth of the Senegal River are similar to the Dungeness type caught in Florida.

8 Dungeness crabs

1/2 cup peanut oil

2 onions, chopped

3 garlic cloves, minced

4 scallions, chopped

1 habanero pepper, chopped

2 cups water

1 bay leaf

2 tablespoons tomato paste

2 bunches curly parsley, finely chopped

Salt and freshly ground black pepper

SERVES 4

1. Wash the crabs well and cut them in half through the middle. Rinse the crabs again.

2. Heat the oil in a large pot over medium heat. Sauté the onions, garlic, scallions, and habanero until soft, about 5 minutes. Add 2 cups water, the bay leaf, tomato paste, and parsley. Cook over medium heat 10 more minutes. Add the crabs, salt, and pepper and steam, covered, 15 minutes. Adjust seasoning and serve hot.

Fried Fish Ragout (Thiou)

In Senegal, it is not uncommon to have a maid, who prepares lunch and dinner on a daily basis. These women are often gifted cooks, as most girls grow up learning the basics of cooking. My friend Amadou Arame is lucky to have an inspired chef as a maid. Every time I am in Senegal, Fatou Bodian prepares Senegalese specialties such as this fried fish ragout from her native Gambia.

1 cup palm oil or canola oil
   (see Glossary)

4 whole snapper (1 1/4 pounds each),
   cleaned and gutted

4 to 5 onions, chopped

3 garlic cloves, minced

3 plum tomatoes, roughly chopped

2 tablespoons tomato paste

1/2 cup dried shrimp, rinsed and
   finely ground in a food processor
   (see Glossary)

1/2 cup dried clams (see Glossary)

3 cups water

1 (2-inch) piece *guedj* (see Glossary)

1 (2-inch) *yet* (see Glossary), or
   substitute 1/4 cup fish sauce for
   both the guedj and yet

1 large yuca, peeled and cut into
   large chunks

2 carrots peeled and cut into chunks

2 sweet potatoes, peeled and
   cut into chunks

1/2 green cabbage cut into large wedges

2 cups whole baby okra

1 tablespoon fresh lime juice

SERVES 4

1. In a large pot over medium heat, heat the palm oil to hot and fry the fish, two at a time, until crisp, about 10 minutes, turning once. Set aside on a warm platter.

2. Meanwhile, combine the onions, garlic, and tomatoes. Sauté in the same oil, over medium heat, until soft, about 5 minutes.

3. Add the tomato paste, dried shrimp, and clams, and stir over low heat. Simmer until the oil starts rising to the surface, about 15 minutes.

4. Add 3 cups water, raise the heat, and bring it to a boil. Add the *guedj* and *yet*, yuca, carrot, sweet potatoes, and cabbage. Reduce the heat and simmer about 15 minutes. Add okra and simmer, 5 minutes. Using a slotted spoon, remove cooked vegetables to a platter. Return fried fish into the pot to heat through, 5 minutes, and sprinkle with the lime juice. Serve hot.

Fish market on the beach in Soumbedioune

Rice and Seafood Pilaf (Kathio)

1 cup palm oil or canola oil (see Glossary)

1 onion, chopped

1 quart water

1 *diaxatou* (see Glossary), or
    1 eggplant, cut into large chunks

2 carrots, peeled and cut into
    large chunks

1 large yuca, peeled and cut into
    large chunks

2 tablespoons fish sauce (see Glossary)

1 fish bouillon cube

2 to 3 whole carp, cleaned and gutted
    (3 pounds total)

1 pound medium shrimp, peeled and
    deveined

2 cups dried oysters, rinsed
    (see Glossary)

1 cup dried shrimp, rinsed and
    finely ground in a food processor
    (see Glossary)

 2 cups rice, preferably traditional Djola
    "red rice" from Casamance; brown rice
    or basmati can be used

SERVES 4

1. In a large pot over medium-low heat, heat the palm oil; add onion and cook until soft. Add 1 quart water; bring to a boil. Add the vegetables and fish sauce; reduce heat and simmer until the vegetables are soft, 15 to 20 minutes. Remove vegetables to a heated platter and cover to keep warm.

2. Dissolve the bouillon cube in the broth and add the fish; simmer gently until cooked, about 15 minutes. Using a spatula, place the cooked fish on the vegetable platter.

3. Add the shrimp, dried oysters, and ground dried shrimp to the pot. Adjust seasoning. Pour the rice into the seafood broth, adding more water if necessary to just cover the rice. Bring to a boil, reduce heat, and simmer, covered tightly, until the rice is tender, about 15 minutes. Fluff the rice with a large spoon and serve in a bowl along with the vegetables and fish. *Kathio* can be eaten with a side of *baguedj* (sorrel-okra puree; see recipe page 68).

Lemon Sole with Green Almond and Smoked Oyster Sauce

Noix de Badamier grow in the Casamance region of Senegal. They have a bitter taste that disappears once cooked. They are reputed to alleviate hypertension—my uncle Joseph swears by this dish as his remedy. You can substitute fresh green almonds, which, when in season, can be found in Middle Eastern shops.

1 cup *noix de Badamier* (or use green almonds)

1 quart water

2 carrots, peeled and cut into large chunks

1 head green cabbage, cut into wedges

1 *diaxatou* (see Glossary), or 1 eggplant, cut into large chunks

1 fish bouillon cube

4 lemon sole fillets (2 pounds total)

1/2 cup dried shrimp, rinsed and ground

1/2 cup dried oysters, rinsed (see Glossary)

4 cups cooked rice (recipe follows)

SERVES 4

1. Using a food processor, grind the nuts to a powder.

2. In a large pot over high heat, bring 1 quart water to a boil. Pour the ground nuts slowly into the boiling water, stirring often to avoid lumps. Reduce heat to medium-low and simmer, partially covered, until the oil separates from the nuts and the sauce thickens, about 25 minutes.

3. Drop the vegetables and the bouillon cube into the broth and continue simmering, 25 to 30 minutes. Using a slotted spoon, remove the vegetables to a heated platter.

4. Drop the fish fillets, the ground dried shrimp, and the smoked oysters into the pot and simmer, about 10 minutes. Adjust seasonings. Combine with reserved vegetables and serve with rice.

Rice (Nyankatang)

If you are unable to locate Djola rice, you can substitute brown or basmati rice. In that case, adjust the recipe to allow for 1 1/2 cups water for every cup of rice.

4 cups water

2 cups rice, preferably Djola "red rice" from Casamance

Salt, to taste

1 (2-inch) piece *guedj* (optional) (see Glossary)

SERVES 8

1. In a medium pot, bring 4 cups water to a boil. Slowly pour the rice into boiling water. Add salt and stir slowly once. Return to a boil, reduce heat, and simmer, tightly covered until all the water evaporates, about 15 minutes.

2. With a spoon, dig a hole in the center of the rice and bury the *guedj* in it. Close the lid and let it sit off the heat, 5 minutes. Transfer rice to a serving bowl and fluff with a fork.

Oyster Elinkine

This simple recipe is from Clarisse Diatta, my cousin's wife in the village of Elinkine. In Casamance, oysters are harvested in abundance from February to the beginning of June. They are either grilled on a wood fire until the shells open or boiled and served with a lime and onion dressing somewhat similar to the classic mignonette. Oysters are also smoked or dried for use as a seasoning for sauces.

4 dozen oysters in shells, well scrubbed to remove sand

2 quarts water

1 onion, thinly sliced

1 habanero pepper, seeded and thinly sliced

1 seafood or chicken bouillon cube, crumbled

Juice of 2 limes

SERVES 4

1. Place the clean oysters in a large pot with the water and bring to a boil. Cook briskly until the shells open. Drain the oysters, reserving 1/4 cup of the cooking water.

2. With a sharp knife, cut the meat from the shells and place in a salad bowl. Add onions, habanero, crumbled bouillon cube, lime juice, and the reserved cooking water. Toss together and adjust seasoning.

Grouper and Millet "Polenta" (Niiri Liidi)

2 pounds grouper fillets (about 6 fillets)

1/2 cup *rof* (recipe follows)

1/4 cup vegetable oil

2 onions, finely chopped

1 cup tomato paste

1 cup coarsely chopped plum tomatoes

4 quarts water

1 carrot, peeled and quartered

2 yuca, peeled and cut into large chunks

2 *diaxatou* (see Glossary), or small European or Japanese eggplants, cut into large chunks

1 handful dried white sorrel flowers (optional)

1 tablespoon fish sauce (see Glossary), or a 2-inch piece *guedj* (see Glossary)

1 habanero pepper

2 pounds coarse millet flour

Lemon, lime, or tamarind juice, to taste

SERVES 8

1. Cut a slit into the flesh of each fish fillet and insert about 1 tablespoon *rof* in each.

2. Heat the oil in a large pot and sauté the onions over medium heat until soft but not brown. Add the tomato paste and chopped tomatoes and let it reduce at medium-low heat, about 10 minutes. Add 4 quarts water and the fish along with the carrot, yuca, eggplant, sorrel flower (if using), and the fish sauce or *guedj*. Bring to a boil, reduce heat, and simmer. Remove the fish and vegetables from the pot as they cook through. Allow the broth to simmer an additional 30 minutes, for flavors to fully develop. Add the habanero towards the end of cooking.

3. Adjust seasonings and slowly pour the millet flour into the cooking liquid, stirring to avoid lumps. Simmer about 30 minutes, stirring occasionally.

4. Add the lemon, lime, or tamarind juice and stir. Serve the millet with the fish and vegetables on the side.

Madjiguene Diaw

Bakary Calamari Salad

This is the most tender calamari salad I've ever had. It was served to me in a quaint hotel in Casamance, "Au Bar de la Mer." I named the salad after the chef, Bakary Diedhiou.

1 1/2 pounds squid

1 tablespoon red wine vinegar, or to taste

2 garlic cloves, minced

1/2 teaspoon salt

1/4 teaspoon fresh ground black pepper

1 cup thinly sliced red onion

1 plum tomato, diced

1/3 cup extra-virgin olive oil

SERVES 4

1. If you've purchased whole squid, clean them first: Gently pull the head and tentacles away from the body, then pull out the backbone from inside the body and discard it along with the intestines and ink sac; cut the tentacles from the head just below the eyes and discard head; remove the membrane from body.

2. Rinse all the squid under running water and pat dry. Cut the tentacle bunches in half, and cut the bodies into 1/4- to 1/3-inch-wide rings; cut the wings from the bodies.

3. Bring 5 to 6 quarts of water to a boil in a large saucepan. Prepare a bowl of ice water.

4. Drop the squid into the boiling water for approximately 5 minutes. Quickly drain and immerse squid in the iced water to stop the cooking. When cooled, strain and dry on a clean towel.

5. Meanwhile, in a small mixing bowl, whisk together the vinegar, garlic, salt, pepper, red onion, and tomato. When the salt dissolves, slowly add the extra-virgin olive oil, whisking constantly. Taste and adjust seasoning.

6. Toss squid with the dressing. Refrigerate for 5 hours before serving (it will become more tender as it marinates in dressing). Toss from time to time. Serve at room temperature.

Fish Stew from Casamance (Caldou)

Djola is the name of my ethnic group—and this dish is a Djola classic. The Djola people live in the southwestern region of Senegal called Casamance and rely largely on tourism and rice cultivation for income. *Caldou* gives an African lilt to the Portuguese name for clear soup, *caldo*. Prepared from simple ingredients, this hearty and pungent dish is a perennial favorite, usually served with white rice and a sorrel-okra condiment called *baguedj* (recipe follows).

2 firm, white-flesh fish (carp, tilapia, or bass) (1 1/2 pounds each)

Salt and freshly ground black pepper

Juice of 2 lemons

3 cups water

2 cups basmati rice

1 tablespoon peanut or canola oil

1 small onion, sliced into 1/4-inch rounds

1 tomato, chopped

1 tablespoon fish sauce (see Glossary) or one 2-inch piece *guedj* (see Glossary)

5 to 6 okra pods (optional)

1 habanero pepper

SERVES 4

1. With a sharp knife, cut 2 or 3 slashes on each side of the fish (about 1 inch deep). Rub salt, pepper, and 1 tablespoon of the lemon juice onto the outside of the fish and inside the slashes. Allow to marinate 1 hour in the refrigerator.

2. Meanwhile, bring 3 cups water to a boil in a pot with a lid. Add the rice, return to a boil, lower the heat, cover and simmer until water is absorbed, 10 to 20 minutes, depending on the variety. Remove from heat.

3. Heat the oil in a large saucepan over medium heat. Sauté the onion and tomato until onion is soft but not brown. Add the fish and enough water to cover. Bring to a boil. Reduce heat and add the fish sauce or *guedj*. Simmer until half-cooked, about 10 minutes. Add the okra pods and the habanero and continue cooking until tender, about 15 minutes. Remove from heat and add the remaining lemon juice to the pan. Serve the fish on a platter with the sauce, vegetables, and rice on the side.

Sorrel-Okra Puree (Baguedj)

4 to 5 okra pods, tops removed

2 bunches sorrel, or substitute 1 bunch spinach plus 1 tablespoon fresh lemon juice

1 tablespoon fish sauce or 2-inch square guedj (see Glossary)

Freshly ground black pepper

MAKES ABOUT 1 CUP

1. In a small saucepan, cook the okra in boiling water until tender, about 5 minutes. Drain and set aside. In a separate pot, over medium heat, cook the sorrel or spinach with a little water and fish sauce (or *guedj*) until soft and wilted, about 5 minutes. Drain.

2. Puree the greens in a blender with the okra and black pepper; if using spinach, blend with 1 tablespoon lemon juice. Pour into a serving bowl.

Steamed Millet with Poached Tilapia (Muuda Joola)

A side of sorrel-okra puree (*baguedj*, see page 68) goes well with *muuda joola*.

2 pounds coarse millet couscous (see Glossary)

1/2 cup vegetable oil

1 cup *rof* (see recipe page 75)

1 cup finely chopped okra

4 whole tilapia (about 1 1/2 pounds each)

1 quart water

1 cup chopped onion

1 cup crushed plum or cherry tomatoes

1 tablespoon fish sauce (see Glossary), or 2-inch piece *guedj* (see Glossary)

2 habanero peppers

Juice of 2 lemons

1 tablespoon freshly ground black pepper

SERVES 8

1. Rinse the millet in water; drain well. Using your fingers or a fork, work about 5 tablespoons oil into the millet to avoid clumps when steaming. Place the millet in the top of a steamer lined with cheesecloth set over medium heat and steam until the millet is completely cooked, about 15 minutes.

2. Add 2 tablespoons *rof* and the okra to the millet and steam about 15 minutes more.

3. Cut the fish in half crosswise, separating the head end from the tail end. With a paring knife, open a slit on the cut sides of each fish and with your finger insert 1 tablespoon *rof* in each.

4. Put the fish in a large pot along with 1 quart water and 2 tablespoons *rof*. Bring to a boil, reduce the heat, and simmer 15 minutes.

5. Add the remaining oil to the pot along with the onions, tomatoes, and fish sauce or *guedj*. Let it simmer for another 15 minutes and then add the habaneros.

6. Remove from the heat and add the lemon juice and black pepper to the broth. Taste and adjust seasonings. Serve with the steamed millet.

Salmon Charmoula

I often serve this dish at parties, substituting one large salmon fillet (4 to 5 pounds) for the steaks. When I do, I leave the salmon to cook in the oven an additional 10 minutes.

1 pound cracked green olives (preferably Greek, packed in brine), pitted and chopped

1/2 cup *charmoula* paste (recipe follows)

4 salmon steaks (1/2 to 3/4 pound each)

2 lemons, peeled and sliced into rounds

1/3 cup water

1/3 cup olive oil

3 to 4 tablespoons fresh lemon juice

SERVES 4

1. Boil the olives for about 5 minutes 3 times, changing the water each time to rid them of bitterness.

2. Rub half of the *charmoula* onto the fish. Let stand 30 minutes.

3. Preheat the oven to 400°F. Place the fish in an ungreased baking pan. Lay the lemon slices neatly over the fish. Mix together the remaining *charmoula* paste, olives, 1/3 cup water, and the oil. Cover the salmon steaks with the olive mixture. Wrap with aluminum foil and bake 15 minutes. Remove the foil and bake 15 minutes more. Sprinkle with lemon juice and serve warm.

Charmoula

Charmoula is of Moroccan origin, one of the many recipes we share with our neighbor north of the Sahara. *Charmoula* works well as a rub for heartier fish such as salmon and on roast meat.

1/2 cup coarsely chopped cilantro leaves

1/2 cup coarsely chopped parsley leaves

4 to 5 garlic cloves, crushed

2 tablespoons white wine vinegar

1/3 cup fresh lemon juice

1 teaspoon salt

1 1/2 teaspoons paprika

2 tablespoons ground cumin

Pinch of ground cayenne pepper

MAKES ABOUT 1 CUP

1. In a blender, combine the herbs, garlic, and vinegar and blend until a paste forms. Place in a mixing bowl and stir in the lemon juice, salt, and spices. Charmoula will keep, refrigerated, for 2 weeks.

Rof

Rof, pronounced "rawf," is a popular condiment in Senegal, commonly used to stuff fish.

1 bunch parsley, coarsely chopped

1 habanero pepper, stemmed and coarsely chopped

3 garlic cloves

1 onion, chopped, or a small bunch of scallions, white parts only, chopped

1 bay leaf, crumbled

Salt and freshly ground black pepper

MAKES ABOUT 1 CUP

1. Place all the ingredients in a food processor and process coarsely, or pound by hand in a mortar and pestle.

Aunt Marie's backyard kitchen

Stuffed Whole Fish (Poisson Farci)

This delicate dish comes from the old colonial town of St. Louis, the same place that gave us *thiebou jen*. To prepare *poisson farci*, you will need a fish that hasn't been gutted yet, as it will be emptied from a cut along the dorsal spine of the fish. It seems tedious, but at the end you are sure to impress your guests with your skill. This dish can be prepared a day in advance, sliced when cold, and warmed before serving.

FOR THE FISH

1 whole mullet, scaled, or any firm white-flesh fish, between 1 1/2 and 2 pounds

1 garlic clove

1 large onion, chopped

1 bunch curly parsley

1/2 bunch cilantro

1 fish bouillon cube

1 teaspoon black peppercorns

2 pinches salt

1/2 pound stale baguette

1 cup milk or water

3 tablespoons peanut oil

1/4 pound small shrimp, shelled and deveined

1/2 cup water

FOR THE SAUCE

1 tablespoon black peppercorns

1 habanero pepper

1 garlic clove

1 large onion, chopped

2 tablespoons peanut oil

1 pound ripe tomatoes, diced

2 tablespoons tomato paste

Salt

1 cup water

1 green bell pepper, diced

SERVES 4

1. Preheat the oven to 325°F. To prepare the fish: With a pair of scissors, cut the fins off the fish and discard. Using a sharp knife, cut just through the skin, on both sides of the dorsal spine of the fish, from head to tail. Pass your fingers between the skin and the flesh to separate the two on both sides of the fish. With your knife or scissors, remove the spine from the head and tail, by cutting at their base. Only the empty skin should remain attached to the head and the tail. Rinse well. With a paring knife, separate the flesh from the bones and innards. Remove the flesh to the bowl of a food processor, and reserve the carcass.

2. Process the fish flesh to a paste with the garlic, onion, parsley, cilantro, bouillon cube, peppercorns, and salt.

3. Soak the stale bread in the milk or water until soft and spongy. Remove and squeeze well with your hands before putting it in the food processor with the fish mixture. Process once more until the mixture is well blended. Remove to a bowl and fold in 2 tablespoons oil until the filling is smooth. Reserve.

4. To make the sauce: Process or pound the black peppercorns, habanero, garlic, and onion to a rough consistency. In a pot, heat 2 tablespoons oil. Add the onion mixture, tomatoes, tomato paste, salt, and 1 cup water. Bring to a boil and reduce the heat; simmer for about 20 minutes. Add the green pepper and simmer for an additional 10 minutes.

5. To assemble the fish: Reshape the fish by filling the carcass with the stuffing. Be careful not to overstuff, as the stuffing will expand in the oven and can burst the skin. Carefully arrange the shrimp on top of the filling before closing the fish skin over it. Sew the fish skin with heavy thread or truss with butcher's twine, brushing the skin with the remaining 1 tablespoon oil.

6. Set the prepared fish on an ungreased cooking tray and pour the sauce over it along with 1/2 cup water. Cover the fish with foil and place it in the oven. Bake for about 30 minutes, basting the fish regularly with the sauce.

7. Remove the whole fish to a serving platter, and cut the thread or butcher's twine with scissors. With a sharp knife, carefully cut 2-inch-long slices across the fish before drizzling all around with the sauce. Serve hot.

Tilapia and Millet Porridge (Gar)

To make vegetarian *gar*, substitute yam, cabbage, carrots, or other vegetables for the fish.

1/4 cup peanut oil

1 large onion, minced

1 pound plum tomatoes, seeded and chopped

4 tilapia steaks (3 pounds total)

1 teaspoon salt

3 cups water

1 tablespoon fish sauce (see Glossary)

1 habanero pepper

1 pound millet couscous or coarse cornmeal

3 tablespoons tamarind or fresh lime juice

SERVES 4

1. Heat the oil in a large pot over medium heat. Add the onions, tomatoes, fish, and salt; stir gently. Let it cook for 5 minutes, then add 3 cups water, the fish sauce, and the habanero. Simmer until the fish is cooked through, about 15 minutes. With a slotted spatula, remove the fish from the cooking broth. Reserve.

2. Slowly pour the millet couscous or cornmeal into the broth, gently whisking to avoid clumps. Simmer 15 minutes. Add the tamarind or lime juice and whisk well to incorporate. Continue cooking until the millet is soft to the bite, about 15 minutes; *gar* should be very moist, with the consistency of a creamy polenta. Serve in a shallow bowl with the fish and habanero on the side.

MEAT

Rack of Venison Baked in Kraft Paper (Dibi Biche)

Dibiteries are small eateries where meat, usually lamb, is prepared as follows. They are popular, affordable hangouts, and the fare is always flavorful.

I had my first *dibi biche* in Cap Skirring, a beautiful resort town near the border with Guinea Bissau. The owner would go hunting for deer during the day and serve his *dibi* at night. Wrapping the meat tightly in brown paper during baking keeps the juices and flavors sealed in. The meat always stays tender this way. Lamb can easily be substituted for the venison.

1 (4- to 6-pound) rack of venison, cut into 2- to 3-inch pieces with a cleaver

1 onion, thinly sliced

1 chicken bouillon cube, crumbled

1 teaspoon freshly ground black pepper

1/2 teaspoon salt

2 garlic cloves, minced

2 sprigs thyme

1/4 cup water

Dijon mustard

1 baguette loaf

SERVES 6

1. Preheat the oven to 450°F. In a large bowl, mix together the meat, onion, bouillon, pepper, salt, garlic, and thyme.

2. Spread a piece of heavy-duty kraft paper wide enough to wrap around the meat on a work surface. Place the prepared meat in the center of the paper. Add the water to the meat before closing paper tight, folding the ends over each other, to seal well.

3. Place the package on a sheet pan and bake 20 to 25 minutes. Adjust seasoning and serve immediately in cooking paper with Dijon mustard and French baguette on the side.

Tripe Stew with Beef and Calf's Feet

3 pounds calf's feet (2 or 3 feet), cut into 3-inch lengths

1 pound tripe, cut into 3-inch squares

2 1/2 quarts water

2 cups finely chopped onions

2 tablespoons finely chopped garlic

1/2 teaspoon cayenne pepper

1 1/2 teaspoons white pepper

2 1/2 teaspoons salt

2 pounds boneless stewing beef, preferably chuck, trimmed of fat and cut into 1 1/2 -inch pieces

1/4 cup peanut oil or vegetable oil

3 firm ripe tomatoes, peeled, seeded, and coarsely chopped, or 1 cup chopped drained canned tomatoes

3 tablespoons tomato paste

1/4 cup dried ground shrimp (see Glossary)

1 habanero pepper

SERVES 8 TO 10

1. Place the calf's feet in a 6- or 8-quart pot and cover them with cold water. Bring the water to a boil and cook them briskly for 2 minutes. Drain and rinse thoroughly under cold running water.

2. Return the calf's feet to the pot along with the tripe and 2 1/2 quarts water. Bring to a boil over high heat. Add 1 cup onions and 1 tablespoon garlic along with the cayenne pepper, white pepper, and 2 teaspoons salt. Simmer, partially covered, 1 1/2 hours. Add the beef and simmer 30 minutes longer.

3. With tongs, transfer the meat to a platter. With a small knife, cut the meat off the calf's feet and discard the fat and bones. Strain the broth through a fine sieve set over a bowl, pressing down hard on the solids, and reserve.

4. Rinse and dry the pot. Heat the oil in it over medium heat, then drop in the remaining 1 cup onions. Cook, stirring frequently, about 5 minutes, until soft but not brown. Add the tomatoes, tomato paste, the remaining 1 tablespoon garlic, the dried ground shrimp, and the remaining 1/2 teaspoon salt. Cook until the mixture is thick, about 5 minutes.

5. Return the meat to the pot and stir in 4 cups of the reserved broth, adding more water if necessary. Add the habanero and return to a boil over high heat. Reduce heat and simmer 1 hour until the meat is very tender when pierced with a knife. Adjust seasoning. Serve with rice (see recipe page 62).

Five-Spice Duck

My grandparents lived in Casamance, the only region in my country with a large Christian presence. For food, they raised both ducks and pigs. Tonton Jean spent much time there, treating us often to his recipe for Vietnamese roast duck, *canard lacqué*. His duck marinade—which can be used on other fowl such as goose, guinea hen, or even chicken—is a perfect blend of sweet and savory, typical of my uncle's heritage, yet new to mine.

16 garlic cloves

8 shallots

1/2 cup sugar

**1 tablespoon five-spice mix
  (recipe follows)**

6 tablespoons fish sauce (see Glossary)

**6 tablespoons sherry or Chinese
  cooking wine**

1 tablespoon vegetable oil

**2 double Muscovy (or magret) duck
  breasts, cut into halves**

SERVES 4

1. Combine the garlic, shallots, sugar, five-spice mix, fish sauce, and sherry in a blender or food processor; blend to a smooth paste.

2. With a sharp knife, cut the skin side of the duck breast in a criss-cross pattern (this will facilitate the release of fat while cooking). In a plastic bag, combine the duck with the marinade and refrigerate for at least 2 hours.

3. Preheat the oven to 375°F. Heat the vegetable oil in a large sauté pan over high heat. Remove the duck from the marinade and drain well. Place the duck in the hot pan, skin side down, and cook 5 minutes; turn once and finish in the oven, about 5 more minutes for medium-rare.

Five-Spice Mix

This Vietnamese spice mix is delicious as a rub on poultry or firm-fleshed fish. It can also be used in marinades.

1 tablespoon ground cinnamon

**2 tablespoons Szechuan peppercorns,
  ground**

1 tablespoon fennel seeds, ground

2 tablespoons star anise, ground

1 teaspoon cloves, ground

MAKES ABOUT 1/3 CUP

1. Blend the spices well and store in an airtight container.

Cornish Hen Farci au Fonio

For centuries, fonio, an ancient, tiny-seeded grain, has been one of our main staples. According to the cosmogony of the Dogon people in Mali, the whole universe emerged from a fonio seed. It was also revered as sacred in ancient Egypt. It was grossly overlooked during our colonial times when the French decided that Senegal's farmland would be used mainly to cultivate peanuts. Now, however, fonio is finding its way back into our bowls and bellies. This is, without a doubt, due to its delicious taste and its nutritional wealth. In fact, fonio is a supergrain, and is still Africa's little secret.

2 cups fonio (see Glossary)

1 tablespoon salt dissolved in 1/4 cup water

2 tablespoons unsalted butter

Salt, to taste

1 carrot, peeled and cut into 1/2-inch cubes

1 cup shelled green peas

1 cup corn kernels

4 Cornish hens, about 1 to 2 pounds each

2 tablespoons *rof* (see recipe page 75)

4 tablespoons Dijon mustard

2 tablespoons white vinegar

2 cups peanut oil

1 onion, julienned

2 green bell peppers, julienned

2 cups water

SERVES 4

1. To prepare the fonio, wash the grains with running cold water and drain well. Place the fonio in the top of a steamer lined with cheesecloth. Set over simmering water, cover, and steam, about 15 minutes. Remove from heat and fluff with a fork. Drizzle with salted water and return the fonio to the steamer basket and steam again until the grains are tender. (Alternatively, fonio can be prepared in a microwave by adding enough water to cover in a bowl and cooking until tender, 6 to 8 minutes.) Add the butter and fold it into the cooked fonio.

2. Meanwhile, place a pot of water over high heat. When it comes to a boil, add salt. Cook the vegetables separately just until tender—the carrots for 15 minutes, the peas for 5 minutes, and the corn for 5 minutes. Drain well and combine the cooked vegetables with the steamed fonio. Set aside.

3. With the tip of a sharp knife, cut a few incisions in the Cornish hens and stuff with some *rof*. Mix together the remaining *rof*, mustard, and vinegar. Season the birds with this mixture. Stuff the cavity of each hen with the fonio, reserving the remaining fonio for serving. Secure with toothpicks or sew with kitchen thread.

4. In a pot large enough to hold the Cornish hens in a single layer, heat the oil and brown the hens for about 15 minutes to a nice golden color. Remove the birds from the pot into a bowl. Pour off all but about 2 tablespoons oil from the pot.

5. Reheat the oil over medium heat. Add the onions and green pepper, stirring until softened but not browned. Return the hens and accumulated juice to the pot along with 2 cups water. Bring to a boil and reduce. Season with salt. Simmer, covered, for about 20 minutes. Serve with the reserved fonio and vegetables, along with the sauce from the cooking pot.

Popping Fonio

In southern Togo, women put a little fonio into a metal pot and swirl it over a fire. Within a few seconds the grains begin bursting and bouncing, and the result is a light and puffy snack like popcorn. Millet seeds can be popped in the same fashion.

Lamb and Vegetable Stew with Millet Couscous

Grilled Chicken with Lime-Onion Sauce (Yassa Ginaar)

10 limes

5 tablespoons peanut oil

2 chicken bouillon cubes, crumbled

5 onions, thickly julienned

Salt and freshly ground black pepper

2 (3-pound) chickens, each cut into 8 pieces

1 cup water

1 habanero pepper

4 cups cooked rice (see recipe page 62)

SERVES 4 TO 6

1. Grate the zest of 3 limes and transfer the zest to a large bowl; juice all 10 limes into the bowl. Add 2 tablespoons oil, the bouillon cubes, onions, salt, and pepper. Rub this mixture into the chicken. Cover and let marinate in the refrigerator for 2 hours, or 1 hour on the counter. Strain the chicken, reserving the marinade juice and onions separately.

2. Preheat a broiler, grill pan, or outdoor grill over high heat. Working in batches, grill the chicken pieces, turning once, until nicely browned. Set aside on a platter.

3. While the chicken is grilling, heat the remaining 3 tablespoons oil in a large pot over medium heat. Add the reserved onions and cook, covered, until caramelized, adding water, 1/4 cup at a time, and stirring occasionally to avoid scorching, 20 to 30 minutes. Add the grilled chicken and juice from the platter along with the marinade and habanero. Season with salt. Bring to a boil, lower the heat, and simmer, covered, until cooked through, about 20 minutes. Transfer the chicken and onion sauce to a platter. Serve with rice.

Lamb and Vegetable Stew with Millet Couscous (Thiere Neverdaye)

This recipe comes from my great-aunt Doubba Kande, whom we affectionately call Mamma. She is of Fulani ancestry. The Fulanis are a nomadic people who harvest millet as their staple. *Thiere neverdaye* is traditionally made with *neverdaye*, a mild-tasting yet tangy indigenous leaf. Here, we substitute with a mix of spinach and cabbage.

2 1/2 pounds lamb shank

1 onion, diced

2 garlic cloves, minced

2 bay leaves

2 quarts plus 1 cup water

2 tablespoons tomato paste

1/2 pound ground peanut flour (see Glossary)

1 head cabbage, julienned

1 habanero pepper

Salt and freshly ground black pepper

1/2 pound spinach, finely chopped

FOR THE COUSCOUS:

1/2 cup dried white beans, soaked overnight

2 cups millet couscous or wheat couscous (if using wheat couscous, follow preparation instructions on the box)

2 tablespoons water

Salt and freshly ground black pepper

SERVES 6

1. Make the stew: In a large pot combine the meat, onion, garlic, and bay leaves. Add 2 quarts water, and bring to a boil; reduce to a simmer. Stew the meat for about 30 minutes.

2. Dilute the tomato paste in the 1 remaining cup water and add to the pot along with the ground peanut flour. Simmer 15 minutes.

3. Meanwhile, cook the cabbage in a separate pot of boiling water until soft, about 10 minutes. Drain well.

4. Add the drained cabbage and the habanero to the stew and stir well. Season generously with salt and pepper. Return to a boil, then lower the heat and let it simmer about 5 minutes. Add the spinach to the stew and stir well. Simmer for 10 minutes.

5. Prepare the couscous: Drain the beans and boil until tender, about 30 minutes. Drain and set aside.

6. Fill the bottom of a steamer with water. Wet the couscous with about 2 tablespoons water. With your fingers, work the couscous until the grains are moistened. Place the couscous in the top of a steamer lined with cheesecloth. Set over simmering water, cover, and steam until soft, about 15 minutes. Off the heat, fold the beans into the couscous and fluff with a fork. Season with salt and pepper.

7. Remove the couscous to a large platter, making a well in the center. Place the meat and vegetables in the center, then ladle the sauce over all. Serve with *kaani* sauce (see recipe page 115), on the side.

Beef Knuckle Soup
(Soupou Yell)

3 pounds beef knuckles

2 bay leaves

2 1/2 quarts water

1 leek, cleaned and chopped

2 cups finely chopped onion

2 tablespoons finely chopped garlic

1 tablespoon black peppercorns

1 beef or chicken bouillon cube

2 pounds boneless stewing beef,
  preferably chuck, trimmed of excess
  fat, and cut into 1 1/2-inch pieces

1/4 cup peanut or vegetable oil

3 large tomatoes, diced, or 1 cup canned
  tomatoes, chopped and drained

3 tablespoons tomato paste

2 1/2 tablespoons salt

1/2 pound Idaho potatoes, peeled
  and cubed

1/2 pound carrots, peeled cut into
  1-inch-thick rounds

2 turnips, peeled and cubed

SERVES 8 TO 10

1. Blanch the beef knuckles in a large pot by covering them with cold water, bringing the water to a boil, and cooking it briskly for 2 minutes. Drain and rinse thoroughly under cold running water.

2. Wash out the pot and return the knuckles to it along with the bay leaves and 2 1/2 quarts water. Bring to a boil.

3. Meanwhile, using a food processor, combine the leek, 1 cup chopped onion, 1 tablespoon chopped garlic, the peppercorns, and bouillon. Add this mixture to the broth. Return to a boil, reduce heat, and simmer for at least 1 1/2 hours. Add the beef and simmer for 20 more minutes.

4. With tongs or a slotted spoon, transfer the beef and knuckles to a platter. Strain the stock through a fine sieve set over a bowl, pressing down with a spoon to extract all the juice before discarding the vegetables, and reserve.

5. Wash out and dry the pot and return it to the stove. Heat the oil over medium heat, and then drop in the remaining 1 cup of onions. Stirring frequently over moderate heat, cook until the onions are soft and translucent but not brown, about 5 minutes.

6. Add the tomatoes, tomato paste, remaining garlic, and salt. Cook briskly, stirring, until most of the liquid has evaporated.

7. Return the beef knuckles and beef to the pot and stir in the reserved stock. Add the potatoes, carrots, and turnips, adding more water if necessary. Bring to a boil over high heat, reduce heat, and simmer partly covered until the meat is tender, about 1 hour. Adjust seasoning and serve hot.

VEGETABLES

Black-Eyed Pea Salad (Salatu Niebe)

Black-eyed peas are native to Africa. They are an excellent source of calcium, folate, and vitamin A, among other nutrients.

1/2 pound black-eyed peas, soaked in water for 1 hour

1 quart water

Salt and freshly ground black pepper

1 tomato, peeled and diced

1 cucumber, seeded and diced

1 red bell pepper, diced

1 bunch scallions, chopped

1/2 bunch flat-leaf parsley, roughly chopped

Juice of 2 limes

1 habanero pepper, seeded and finely chopped

1 cup extra-virgin olive oil

Lettuce leaves, for serving

SERVES 8

1. Boil the black-eyed peas gently in 1 quart water, 30 minutes. Add salt toward the end of the cooking time. Strain and set aside.

2. In a bowl, mix the tomato, cucumber, bell pepper, scallions, parsley, lime juice, habanero, salt, and pepper. Gradually pour in the oil while whisking. Pour the dressing over the black-eyed peas, folding gently. Allow to sit for 1 hour. Serve nestled in lettuce leaves.

Steamed Fonio and Crushed Peanuts with Spicy Eggplant (Djouka de Fonio)

1 cup raw shelled peanuts

1 cup fonio (see Glossary)

1 tablespoon salt dissolved in
   1/4 cup water

1/2 cup finely sliced okra

1/2 cup water

2 large eggplants, cut into 3-inch chunks

1 habanero pepper

2 tablespoons peanut oil

1 large onion, finely diced

1 garlic clove, minced

Salt, to taste

1 tablespoon freshly ground black pepper

1 tablespoon white vinegar

SERVES 4

1. Finely crush the peanuts using a food processor.

2. Place the fonio in the top of a steamer lined with cheesecloth. Set over simmering water, cover, and steam the fonio, 10 minutes. Drizzle with salted water, using a fork to fluff. Steam 5 more minutes. With the fonio still in the basket, top with the ground peanuts and return to steam for another 10 minutes until well moistened.

3. Meanwhile, in a small pot, bring 1/2 cup water to a simmer and cook okra, 15 to 20 minutes. Combine okra with fonio mixture. Set aside, covered, to keep warm.

4. Place the eggplants and habanero pepper in a small pot with just enough water to cover and bring to a boil; reduce heat and simmer until the eggplants are soft, 15 minutes.

5. Heat the oil in a large sauté pan over medium heat. Add the onions, garlic, salt, and pepper. Cook until the onions are soft, 5 minutes. Add the eggplant and habanero along with their cooking liquid. Stir in the vinegar.

6. Serve the fonio on a platter with the eggplant-onion mixture on top. For a less-spicy version, omit the habanero.

Roasted Pepper Salad (Salata Mechouia)

3 green bell peppers

4 large tomatoes, peeled, seeded, and chopped

1 garlic clove, crushed

Pinch of sweet paprika

1 teaspoon ground cumin

2 tablespoons extra-virgin olive oil

1 tablespoon fresh lemon juice

1 teaspoon freshly ground black pepper

2 preserved lemons (see Glossary)

SERVES 4

1. Over an open flame on the stovetop, roast the peppers with tongs, turning often, until their skins are blackened and blistering. Do not overchar. Alternatively, roast under a hot broiler, turning with tongs, until completely blackened. Place the charred peppers in a brown paper bag, close and set aside to cool. When cool, remove the peppers, core, seed, and slip off their skins. Scrape off all seeds. Cut the flesh into small strips.

2. Mix the tomatoes and peppers in a bowl, then add all the other ingredients except the preserved lemon. Mix well.

3. Rinse the preserved lemons under running water and cut away the pulp. Cut the peel into small cubes and sprinkle over the salad. Serve at room temperature.

Peeled black-eyed peas

Black-Eyed Pea and Sweet Potato Ragout (Ndambe)

1 pound black-eyed peas, soaked in water for 1 hour

1 quart water

Salt and freshly ground black pepper

1 tablespoon vegetable oil

1 onion, finely chopped

1/2 pound plum tomatoes, chopped

1 pound sweet potatoes, cut into 1-inch cubes

SERVES 8

1. Boil the black-eyed peas gently in 1 quart water, 30 minutes. Add salt toward the end of the cooking time. Strain and set aside.

2. In a sauté pan over medium-low heat, heat the oil and sauté the onion until softened. Add the chopped tomatoes and allow to reduce, 5 to 10 minutes. Add the sweet potato cubes and enough water to cover. Simmer until the sweet potatoes are soft. Season, and add the black-eyed peas. Taste, adjust the seasoning, and allow to simmer 10 more minutes before serving.

Grilled Sweet Potatoes

2 pounds sweet potatoes

Vegetable oil

Salt

SERVES 4

1. Preheat a grill pan or outdoor grill over high heat. Wash the sweet potatoes. Bring a pot of water to a boil; add salt. Boil the sweet potatoes, skin on, until just tender, about 15 to 20 minutes. Drain and let cool.

2. With a sharp knife, cut the sweet potatoes into thick rounds and brush the cut sides with a little oil. Place the sweet potato slices on the grill and cook until softened and lightly browned. Serve hot, as a side dish with grilled lamb or fried chicken, or just as is with a spicy sauce, such as the Senegalese *kaani* sauce (see recipe page 115).

West African Yam Paste Balls (Fufu)

Fufu is not native to Senegal, but throughout the forest region of western and central Africa it is part of the daily diet. In addition to yam, *fufu* can be made from yuca, coco yam (taro), or plantain and is a standard accompaniment to spicy soups, stews, and sauces such as *soupou kandja* (see recipe page 130).

1 1/2 pounds yam, peeled and cut into chunks

2 cups water

2 teaspoons salt

SERVES 4

1. Combine the yam, water, and salt in a saucepan and bring to a boil over high heat. Reduce the heat to low, cover the pan tightly, and cook until the yam is tender enough to be easily mashed with a fork, 30 to 45 minutes. Drain the slices in a large colander or sieve. Puree through a food mill set over a bowl.

2. Continue to break down the yam by pounding it with a pestle or a wooden mallet. After every few strokes, dip your pestle into cold water to keep the yam moist and to prevent it from sticking to the pestle. Continue pounding for about 10 minutes until the yam forms a compact but slightly sticky paste.

3. To shape the *fufu* into balls, fill a mixing bowl with cold water and set beside a large plate. Sprinkle a little water on the plate and moisten your hands lightly. Lift up about 1/4 cup yam paste and roll it with your palm across the plate until it is smooth and firm and its surface is shiny. Keep moistening your hands and the plate again from time to time as you roll all the *fufu* balls. You should have about 10 balls.

4. Arrange the *fufu* balls attractively on a platter and serve immediately or wrap with foil and set them aside at room temperature for up to 2 hours before serving.

Vegetable Mafe

Mafe, pronounced "mafay," is of Malian origin, although all of West Africa claims it. It's usually prepared with chicken, fish, or lamb. I've adapted the traditional recipe here for our vegetarian regulars at the restaurant.

1/4 cup peanut oil

1 1/2 onions, diced

2 garlic cloves, very finely minced

2 heaping tablespoons tomato paste

4 1/2 cups water

1 bay leaf

1 vegetable bouillon cube

Salt

1 small cabbage, cut into 6 wedges

1 1/2 pounds tubers of choice: yuca, yam, coco yam, eddoes, potato, etc., peeled and cut into large chunks

1/2 pound butternut squash, peeled and cut into large chunks

2 turnips, peeled and quartered

1 habanero pepper

4 heaping tablespoons smooth peanut butter

10 to 20 okra pods, stemmed and cut widthwise into 1/8-inch rounds or left whole (see Note)

4 cups cooked rice (see recipe page 62)

SERVES 6

NOTES ON INGREDIENTS
The vegetable ingredients can vary according to taste and availability, though the butternut squash is a must. If you slice the okra thinly, they will dissolve into the sauce, giving it that typical, viscous okra texture (which I love). Leaving them whole adds color and the flavor of a second nonstarchy vegetable. For those not too keen on okra, use fewer pods.

1. Heat the oil in a large soup pot, 1 1/2-gallon capacity or more. Add half the onions and half the minced garlic and cook over low heat until soft but not brown.

2. Dilute the tomato paste in 1/2 cup water and add to the pot. Cook over medium-low heat, stirring frequently until the sauce is thickened and the oil glistens on the surface, about 5 minutes. Add 4 cups water and bring to a boil.

3. Add the bay leaf and the bouillon cube, and salt to taste. Stir well to dissolve the bouillon. Add the cabbage, tubers, butternut squash, turnips, and habanero. Return to a boil. Lower the heat to a simmer and cook, removing the vegetables as they become tender, but not mushy. (The butternut squash will be the first to cook, about 20 minutes.) Taste and adjust seasonings as necessary while the vegetables cook. The liquid will reduce to about 3 cups.

4. Remove about 1 cup of liquid and dissolve the peanut butter in it. Pour back into the pot and add the remaining onion and garlic plus the okra. Bring to a boil, reduce to a simmer, and let cook for 10 minutes more, stirring to make sure the sauce is smooth.

5. Arrange the cooked rice on a platter or in a large bowl. Distribute the vegetables over the rice, leaving the habanero on the side where it can easily be seen. Then generously spread the sauce over the vegetables and rice and serve.

Steamed Black-Eyed Pea Puree with Eggplant (Abala)

2 cups dried black-eyed peas, soaked overnight

2 tablespoons palm oil or canola oil (see Glossary)

1 small onion, diced

2 Japanese eggplants, cubed

Salt and freshly ground black pepper

1 large banana leaf, cut into about six 6- to 8-inch squares

SERVES 4 TO 6

1. Rinse the peas, then let them sit for 10 minutes in a large bowl. Peel them by rubbing the soaked peas between the palms of your hands to remove the skins, which will float up to the top. Continue this process, placing the bowl under slowly running water; this will allow the skins to rise to the surface, leaving the beans in the bottom. Alternatively, place the soaked, strained peas in a processor and pulse a few times. Do not attempt to make a paste of the peas. Place the peas in a bowl and fill with water. Then pour the water out through a strainer. The skins, lighter than the peas, will pour out with the water, leaving the peas in the bowl.

2. In a food processor, puree the peeled black-eyed peas.

3. Heat the palm oil in a saucepan over medium-high heat, and sauté the onions until soft. Add the eggplant and cook over medium heat 5 minutes or until the eggplant is cooked through. Season with salt and pepper. Allow to cool.

4. Fold the eggplant mixture into the black-eyed pea puree. Adjust seasoning.

5. Place 2 tablespoons of the mixture in the middle of each banana leaf square. Close the leaf by folding the ends over. Secure with toothpicks or tie with kitchen twine.

6. Place the packets in the top of a steamer and steam 15 to 20 minutes. Serve hot.

Fried Yuca (Yuca Frites)

2 pounds yuca, peeled and cut into large wedges

Vegetable oil, for deep-frying

Salt and freshly ground black pepper

SERVES 4

1. Boil the yuca in water over high heat until soft. Drain.

2. Heat 3 to 4 inches of oil in a deep pan until it reaches 365°F. Drop a few yuca wedges into the oil and fry until golden brown, about 5 minutes. Remove and drain on paper towels. Repeat until all the yuca is fried. Season with salt and pepper and serve hot with Mango Ketchup (recipe follows).

Mango Ketchup

The inspiration for this recipe comes from one for apple ketchup I'd found many years ago during one of my frequent immersions in vintage American cookbooks. It's a great summer dip for crudités and goes notably well over grilled fish. A large peach or a papaya can be substituted for the mango.

1 ripe mango, peeled, pitted, and roughly chopped

1 inch ginger root, peeled and minced

1 teaspoon brown sugar

1 tablespoon soy sauce

1 tablespoon white wine vinegar

4 drops Tabasco sauce

1/4 cup ketchup

MAKES ABOUT 1 CUP

1. Combine all ingredients except the ketchup in a pot and simmer until thickened. Place the mixture plus the ketchup in a food processor and process until smooth. Cover and refrigerate. Mango ketchup will keep for 2 weeks, refrigerated.

Fonio Taboule

This fresh salad is a variation of the Lebanese bulgur salad. It is a healthier version thanks to the nutrient-rich fonio.

1 cup fonio (see Glossary)

**1 tablespoon salt dissolved in
    1/4 cup water**

Juice of 2 lemons

1 teaspoon salt

1/2 teaspoon freshly ground black pepper

1 cup extra-virgin olive oil

1 bunch curly parsley, finely chopped

1 bunch mint, finely chopped

1 cucumber, peeled and diced

1 red bell pepper, diced

2 plum tomatoes, diced

1/2 cup small green olives

SERVES 4

1. Wash the fonio with cold running water and drain well. Place the fonio in the top of a steamer lined with cheesecloth. Set over simmering water, cover, and steam the fonio, about 15 minutes. Remove from heat, and fluff with a fork. Drizzle with salted water and steam again until the grains are tender. (Alternatively, fonio can be prepared in a microwave by adding enough water to cover in a bowl and cooking until tender, 6 to 8 minutes.)

2. In a small mixing bowl, combine the lemon juice with the salt and pepper and whisk to dissolve. Slowly pour in the olive oil, whisking to emulsify.

3. Place the cooked fonio in a large bowl and add parsley, mint, cucumber, red bell pepper, and tomatoes. Pour enough dressing over fonio mixture to coat the grains well. Toss, and serve garnished with olives.

THE MIDDLE PASSAGE

What we know as American Southern cuisine actually has its roots in Africa. Enslaved Africans, to whom the world owes a large debt, kept their culinary traditions alive by bringing ingredients such as yams (*nyami* in Wolof), okra (*gombo*), rice, sesame, and peanuts, to name a few, across the Atlantic during the Middle Passage. Thus we have gumbo in New Orleans, hoppin' John and jambalaya in Louisiana, bene snacks (sesame crackers) in Charleston, red rice in the Gullah Islands, and fish croquettes in the Helena Islands of South Carolina.

Black-Eyed Pea Fritters (Accara)

"Ku begue accara day gneme kaani" ("To enjoy accara one must also endure the hot pepper sauce.")—a Wolof proverb

Accara! This is my favorite street food. These crunchy fritters bring back memories of a special time of the day: *takussan.* It's the time when the singing voice of the *muezzin* can be heard throughout the city, calling the Muslim faithful to prepare for the third of the five daily prayers. The last rays of sun are slowly setting on the Atlantic horizon, and, somehow, that's when I crave *accara* the most. Still. As a child, I would wait religiously every day by Madame Kodjo's stall to purchase her freshly fried *accara.* A native of the tiny West African nation called Benin, Madame Kodjo had achieved that perfect combination of crunchy crust surrounding the perfectly smooth and light bean paste. She would always serve it wrapped in *Le Soleil* or another local newspaper.

Today, *accara* are found wherever West Africans live: from the streets of Lagos and Cotonou or Lomé and Abidjan in Africa, to the shores of Bahia, Brazil, where they're known as *acarajé.* On the Caribbean island of Martinique, *accra* are made of salt cod instead of peas, while in Haiti, they are made with the tuber *malanga.*

1 cup dried black-eyed peas

2 tablespoons coarsely chopped onion

1 teaspoon baking soda

1/2 teaspoon salt, or to taste

1 quart peanut oil, for frying

***Kaani* sauce (recipe follows)**

MAKES ABOUT 20 FRITTERS

1. Soak the peas in warm water for 10 minutes. Rinse the peas, then let them sit for another 10 minutes in a large bowl. Peel them by rubbing the soaked peas between the palms of your hands to remove the skins, which will float up to the top. Continue this process, placing the bowl under slowly running water; this will allow the skins to rise to the surface, leaving the peas in the bottom.

Alternatively, place the soaked, strained peas in a processor and pulse a few times. Do not attempt to make a paste of the peas. Fill the bowl with water. Then pour the water out through a strainer. The skins, lighter than the peas, will pour out with the water, leaving the peas in the bowl.

Soak the peeled peas overnight at room temperature to slightly ferment them.

2. Process or blend the peeled peas, along with the onions, baking soda, and salt, adding a little water to make a smooth paste. Use as little water as possible, the batter should be smooth and light. Taste the seasonings and adjust.

3. In a large frying pan, heat the oil to 365°F. Reduce the heat to medium and drop 1 tablespoonful *accara* batter into the oil. Repeat until there are several dollops in the pan. Do not crowd the pan. Turn fritters once. Remove from the heat when they are golden brown, and drain on paper towels. Serve with *kaani* sauce.

Kaani Sauce

1 onion, coarsely chopped

1 garlic clove, chopped

1 tablespoon peanut oil

6 ripe roma tomatoes, coarsely chopped, or 3 tablespoons tomato paste

1 habanero pepper

1 bay leaf

Salt and freshly ground black pepper

MAKES ABOUT 1 CUP

1. In a saucepan over medium-low heat, sauté the chopped onion and garlic in hot oil until soft and fragrant. Add tomatoes, habanero, and bay leaf. Simmer for 30 minutes, stirring with a wooden spoon. Add salt and pepper. Blend or process until smooth. Taste for zing—the spicier the better!

Rice and Black-Eyed Peas (Thiebou Niebe)

Thiebou niebe became Hoppin' John in the New World. This version comes from the North of Senegal.

1/4 cup peanut oil

1 onion, minced

5 tablespoons tomato paste

3 plum tomatoes, roughly chopped

1 teaspoon salt

2 tablespoons *nokos* (recipe follows)

2 quarts water

1/4 pound dried black-eyed peas, soaked for at least 1 hour

1 cabbage, quartered

6 carrots, peeled and halved

1/2 pound yuca, peeled and cut into large chunks

3 to 4 tablespoons fish sauce (or *guedj* or *yet*) (see Glossary)

2 eggplants, quartered

1 butternut squash, peeled, quartered, and seeded

6 okra pods, trimmed

2 habanero peppers

3 cups broken rice, or whole basmati, soaked for at least 1 hour

SERVES 6

1. In a large pot, heat the oil over medium heat. Add the onion, tomato paste, and chopped tomatoes. Stir well and add the salt and *nokos*. Cover and simmer about 15 minutes on medium-low heat. Pour in about 2 quarts water, cover again, and bring to a boil.

2. Drain the black-eyed peas and add them along with the cabbage, carrots, yuca, and fish sauce, to the pot. Simmer about 30 minutes. Add the eggplant, butternut squash, okra, and habaneros, and simmer until tender, about 10 minutes. Adjust seasonings to taste.

3. Meanwhile, prepare the rice by steaming it over the stew in a steamer basket lined with cheesecloth for about 30 minutes, covered.

4. With a slotted spoon, remove the vegetables to a serving platter, reserving 2 ladlefuls of the sauce.

5. To serve, arrange the rice on a platter, surround with the vegetables, and ladle the reserved sauce over the rice.

Fatou preparing to pound peanuts and rice in a traditional mortar and pestle

Nokos

This is a special seasoning blend used extensively in Wolof households.

1 garlic clove

1 small onion, chopped

4 chicken or vegetable bouillon cubes

1/2 habanero pepper

2 pinches salt

1/2 teaspoon whole black peppercorns

MAKES 1/2 CUP

1. In a mortar and pestle or a food processor, mix all the ingredients to a paste.

Rice and Peas
(Sinan Kussak)

This version of rice and peas is a specialty from the village of Diakene Djola, located in the southern region of Casamance. There, *sinan kussak* is made with palm oil and black-eyed peas that have been peeled.

1 cup dried black-eyed peas

1 quart water

1 1/2 cups Djola rice (see note)

1/2 onion

1 habanero pepper (optional)

1/2 cup palm oil or canola oil
  (see Glossary)

1-inch square *guedj*, or 2 tablespoons
  fish sauce (see Glossary)

SERVES 4

1. Soak the peas in warm water for 10 minutes. Rinse the peas, then let them sit for another 10 minutes in a large bowl. Peel them by rubbing the soaked peas between the palms of your hands to remove the skins, which will float up to the top. Continue this process, placing the bowl under slowly running water; this will allow the skins to rise to the surface, leaving the peas in the bottom. Alternatively, place the soaked, strained peas in a processor and pulse a few times. Do not attempt to make a paste of the peas. Fill the bowl with water. Then pour the water out through a strainer. The skins, lighter than the peas, will pour out with the water, leaving the peas in the bowl.

2. In a large pot, bring 1 quart water and black-eyed peas to a boil. Lower heat and simmer until tender, about 30 minutes.

3. Add the rice and simmer, covered, 15 minutes.

4. In a blender, combine the onion, habanero, and *guedj* (or fish sauce, if using). Add the onion mixture to the pot. With a large spoon, fold in the onion mixture once. Cover the pot and return to simmer for another 15 minutes. Fold in palm oil until the rice has a deep red color.

NOTE: Also called red rice due to the tints of red from the bran, *Djola* rice originates from the south of Senegal and is particularly rich in nutrients. Basmati rice can be used instead.

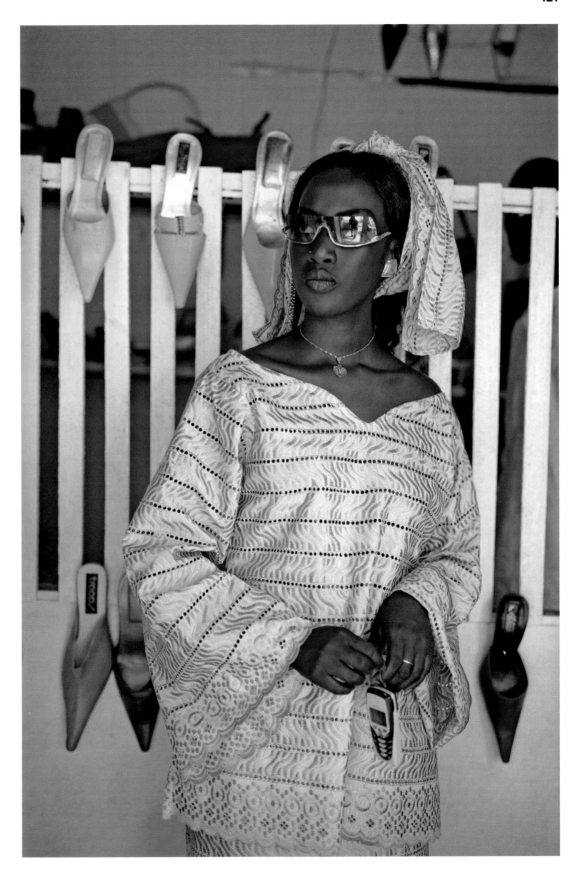

Yuca Couscous Salad (Athieke Salad)

There's a definite relation here to the Lebanese cold grain "salad," taboule. *Athieke* salad was influenced by the many Lebanese who have lived in Dakar for generations, mostly as textile merchants. *Athieke* is yuca (also known as cassava), dried and processed into small grains. It can be served warm or cold as a side dish with grilled fish. In Brazil, this dish is known as *farofa*.

SERVES 6

3 tomatoes, chopped

1 cucumber, peeled and diced

1 bunch scallions, white and tender green stalks only, chopped

1/4 pound dried shrimp (optional) (see Glossary)

Juice of 6 limes (about 3 tablespoons)

1/2 cup olive oil

1 red bell pepper, diced

1 jalapeño pepper, seeded and minced

Salt and freshly ground black pepper

1/2 pound cooked yuca couscous (*athieke*; see Glossary)

Lettuce leaves, for serving

1. In a bowl, mix tomatoes, cucumber, scallions, dried shrimp, lime juice, oil, red pepper, jalapeño, salt, and pepper. Add the yuca couscous, blend well with a wooden spoon, and let sit for 1 hour.

2. To serve, arrange in individual servings on lettuce leaves.

Mme Henriette Vieyra-Sambou grilling chicken for yassa

Blue Fish with Red Rice and Vegetables (Thiebou Jen)

Thiebou jen—in Wolof, "rice with fish"—or just *thieb,* is our national dish. In Africa thieb has become nearly synonymous with Senegal. *Thiebou ginaar* (rice with chicken) and *thiebou yapp* (rice with meat, usually lamb) are also popular, but there's something about the melding of the fish, which we stuff, and the vegetables, cooked in thick tomato sauce, that makes *thiebou jen* memorable. Traditionally, broken rice is used, a holdover from poverty days when the broken rice bits at the bottom of the sacks were usually all that were left come the time to prepare *thiebou jen*.

Often, there will be a coating of browned rice on the pot bottom *(khogn)*, stuck thanks to the sugary thickness of the tomato paste in the sauce. Because these dregs are so delicious, they become the cook's prize, a fitting reward for a hard day's work, which she may or may not choose to share.

Thieb has come to represent to me Senegal's ability to take cuisines from various cultures and put its definitive stamp of ownership on them. The cabbage and carrots were introduced from Europe, and tomatoes, which have become significant in our cuisine, have a New World origin.

2 cups broken white rice or regular basmati rice

1/2 cup peanut oil

2 large onions, diced

1 plum tomato, peeled and chopped, or 1/4 cup finely chopped canned tomatoes (pulp only)

1 cup tomato paste

6 cups water

1 generous pinch sugar

Salt and freshly ground black pepper

5 pounds whole blue fish or other firm, white-flesh fish, cut into 10 steaks about 1 1/2 inches thick, heads reserved

7 tablespoons *rof* stuffing for the fish steaks (see recipe page 75)

1 bay leaf

1/2 large green cabbage, cut into 3 wedges

2 large carrots, peeled and cut into thirds

1 (1-pound) yuca, peeled and cut into thirds

1 small butternut squash, peeled and cut into large chunks or wedges

12 okra pods

1 habanero pepper

1 tablespoon tamarind paste, diluted in 1/4 cup water (see Glossary)

4 to 5 tablespoons fish sauce (see Glossary)

2 limes, cut into wedges, for garnish

SERVES 10

Directions on following page

1. Wash the rice well under cold running water until the water runs clear. (This will eliminate the extra starch and will make the rice less sticky.)

2. Heat the oil in a large pot over medium-low heat. Sauté the onions until soft but not brown, stirring occasionally with a wooden spoon. Add the tomato and stir. Dilute the tomato paste in 1 cup of the water and add to the pot; stir well. Add the sugar and a pinch of salt, and stir to dissolve. Cover the pot and reduce the heat. Simmer until the oil rises above the tomato mixture, stirring occasionally and adding water if needed, 1/2 cup at a time, about 30 minutes. Make sure the tomato does not stick to the bottom of the pot.

3. Meanwhile, season the fish with salt and pepper. Make two 2-inch-long slits in each steak, and stuff each crevice with about 1 teaspoon *rof*.

4. Add the remaining 5 cups water and the bay leaf to the pot. Season to taste with salt and pepper. Carefully place the stuffed fish steaks in the broth, along with the fish heads and the cabbage, carrots, yuca, butternut squash, and okra. Add the habanero. Bring to a boil, then lower to a simmer. Cook uncovered for about 1 hour over medium heat, removing the fish after about 30 minutes and vegetables as they cook through, when they are easily pierced with a knife.

5. Add the tamarind paste to the broth. Adjust the seasonings and let simmer 20 more minutes until oil rises to the surface of the broth.

6. Remove a few ladles of broth to a separate bowl and add the fish sauce. Stir well. Taste the sauce and adjust seasoning again. Remove the habanero, unless you prefer an extra spicy *thieb*.

7. Add the rice to the pot, returning some of the reserved liquid to the pot if necessary, to just cover the rice. Bring to a boil and reduce heat to low. Cover the pot with a tight lid and cook until tender, about 30 minutes.

8. Arrange the rice on a platter, then distribute the vegetables and fish evenly over the rice. Sparingly, spoon some of the reserved cooking liquid over the *thiebou jen* before serving. Serve with lime wedges.

Fish Croquettes (Boulettes)

St. Helena island, off the coast of South Carolina, is an important part of African-American history, and remains a center of Gullah culture today. The origin of the fish croquettes you'll find there can be traced back to Senegalese *boulettes*. The *boulettes* can be cooked ahead of time and warmed in the oven before serving.

FOR THE BOULETTES

4 garlic cloves

1 habanero pepper, seeded and chopped (optional)

2 onions, roughly chopped

2 scallions, white and light green stalks only, roughly chopped

1 bunch parsley, stemmed and roughly chopped

Salt and freshly ground black pepper

1 vegetable or fish bouillon cube

2 pounds firm, white flesh fish fillets, such as snapper, bass, or grouper

1/2 cup breadcrumbs

1/4 cup water or milk

Peanut oil, for frying

FOR THE SAUCE

2 onions, roughly chopped

1 garlic clove

2 tablespoons black peppercorns

1 fish bouillon cube

3 tablespoons peanut oil

3 ripe plum tomatoes, roughly chopped

2 tablespoons tomato paste

2 sprigs thyme

1 bay leaf

1 habanero pepper

2 cups water

SERVES 4

1. To make the *boulettes:* Using a mortar and pestle or a food processor, pound or mix the garlic, habanero (if using), onions, and scallions, along with the parsley, salt, pepper, and bouillon cube until well blended. Remove onion mixture and set aside.

2. Cut the fish into small cubes and pound or process until smooth. Add the reserved onion mixture, breadcrumbs, and water or milk. Stir well to blend, and adjust seasonings.

3. Lightly oil your hands and shape the mixture into walnut-size rounds.

4. Pour about 1 inch oil into a large sauté pan. Heat the oil over medium-high to 375°F. Add the boulettes and deep-fry until nicely brown, about 5 minutes. Serve with sauce and sliced baguettes or other crusty French bread.

5. To make the sauce: Pound the onions, garlic, peppercorns, and bouillon cube using a mortar and pestle or process roughly in a food processor.

6. In a pot, heat the oil over medium heat; add the onion mixture, and slowly sauté 3 to 4 minutes. When the onions are soft, add the chopped tomato and tomato paste (after loosening the paste with a little water). When the sauce begins to simmer, add the thyme, bay leaf, and habanero. Let simmer a few minutes before adding about 2 cups water. Stir and let simmer an additional 30 minutes.

Soupi Kandja Royale

A true ancestor of the Louisiana gumbo, *soupi kandja* is one of those dishes found throughout West and Central Africa. There are many versions of *soupi kandja,* but this is the royal one laden with both seafood and meat, our version of *terra e mare*, or surf 'n turf. The more everyday *soupi kandja* goes easier on the meat and is more closely related to the famed New Orleans shrimp gumbo.

1/2 cup dried shrimp (see Glossary)

1/2 cup dried oysters (optional)
    (see Glossary)

2 pounds beef shoulder, cubed

4 mutton feet (optional)

3 onions, chopped

2 bay leaves

1/2 pound *kong* (or substitute smoked
    catfish, smoked chicken, or turkey leg)

1 pound large shrimp, cleaned and
    deveined

4 crab claws

2 fish bouillon cubes

2 habanero peppers

1/4 pound okra, finely sliced or blended
    to a paste

1/4 cup fish sauce (see Glossary)

1/4 cup palm oil or canola oil (see
    Glossary)

Salt and freshly ground black pepper

4 cups cooked rice (see recipe page 62)

SERVES 8

1. Soak the dried shrimp and dried oysters, if using, in enough water to cover, 30 minutes. Drain and set aside.

2. In a large saucepan over medium heat place beef cubes, mutton feet (if using), onions, and bay leaves. Add enough water to cover. Bring to a boil, reduce the heat to a simmer, and cook about 40 minutes, stirring occasionally and skimming off the foam.

3. Add smoked catfish (or smoked chicken or turkey leg), shrimp, crab claws, bouillon cubes, dried shrimp, and dried oysters. Stir to dissolve the bouillon. Bring to a simmer and add habaneros, okra, fish sauce, palm oil, salt, and pepper. Let the liquid reduce until it's the consistency of clotted cream, about 20 minutes more. Adjust the seasonings. Serve with rice.

Swiss Chard and Beef Stew (Plassas)

No doubt! Aunt Marie Mathiam makes the best *plassas*, a warming, smoky stew of Senegalese greens and chunks of beef. She has three different versions in which she uses either *boro-boro*, yuca leaves, or sweet potato leaves. Swiss chard is a good substitute for these greens. *Plassas* is often prepared with both meat and fish, which I have done here. In the Caribbean, this dish evolved into the popular *calalou*.

2 quarts water

2 pounds beef shoulder, cubed

2 cups peanut butter

2 onions, finely chopped

**1 cup dried shrimp, washed well and
    ground (see Glossary)**

2 to 3 bunches scallions, finely chopped

**1 *kong* (or substitute 1 smoked
    chicken leg or 1 smoked turkey leg)
    (see Glossary)**

**2 bunches swiss chard, stemmed and
    chopped**

2 *diaxatou* (optional) (see Glossary)

5 okras, finely chopped

2 habanero peppers

1 cup palm oil or canola oil (see Glossary)

4 cups cooked rice (see recipe page 62)

SERVES 6

1. In a large pot, bring 2 quarts water to a boil and add meat, peanut butter, and 1/2 of the chopped onion. Reduce heat, cover, and simmer 20 minutes, stirring often.

2. Add dried shrimp, scallions, and remaining chopped onion along with the *kong* (or smoked chicken or turkey leg). Simmer, covered, 10 minutes. Add swiss chard and *diaxatou* (if using) and simmer 10 more minutes. Add chopped okra, habaneros, and palm oil and simmer another 10 minutes. Adjust seasoning and serve with rice.

DESSERTS

Roasted Mango and Coconut Rice Pudding (Sombi)

Sombi is the original after-school comfort food, and for grown-ups, our favorite late-night snack. The success of this dessert lies in its balance of flavors. Just a hint of lime provides a tangy crisp contrast to the woodsy taste of coconut, while both enhance the flavor of the rice. It is fitting that this dessert comes from Casamance, where rice cultivation is the region's lifeblood. You feel a special silence around the paddies at sunset as the rice shoots sway, captives of the gentle breeze. The tranquility of that scene is one of my most vivid memories of home.

1/2 cup honey

2 mangoes, peeled and sliced lengthwise

2 cups coconut milk

1/4 cup sugar, or to taste

1 vanilla bean cut in half lengthwise, seeds scraped out and discarded, or 1 teaspoon vanilla extract

1/2 cup shredded coconut, preferably fresh

1 cup cooked white rice, preferably long-grain

1 pinch salt

1 tablespoon fresh lime juice

SERVES 4 TO 6

1. In a sauté pan over medium heat, cook the honey until bubbly. Add the mango slices and glaze until they are well coated and golden brown, about 5 minutes. Remove from the heat.

2. In a saucepan, combine the coconut milk, sugar, vanilla, and all but 2 tablespoons of the shredded coconut. Cook over medium heat, stirring frequently, until the coconut milk is infused with the other flavors, about 10 minutes. Remove 1/2 cup coconut sauce to a bowl and set aside.

3. Place the remaining shredded coconut in a dry pan over low heat for 5 minutes, shaking the pan occasionally. Set aside.

4. Add the rice to the coconut sauce in the pot and cook slowly, stirring frequently until all the liquid is absorbed. Add the salt and lime juice. Remove from heat and discard the vanilla bean (if using).

5. Divide the rice pudding among 4 to 6 individual dessert bowls, spooning the rice into the center of the bowl and surrounding it with a pool of the reserved coconut sauce. Fan the mango slices over the rice and strew with the toasted coconut. Drizzle any remaining warm honey over the *sombi* for added sweetness. Serve warm.

Windows of Dakar

Paris-Dakar: Apple-Mango Tart

My friend, Zucco, who has a French bistro (Zucco) on Manhattan's trendy Lower East Side, came up with the name for this dessert. He thought I should create a signature dish bridging France and Senegal. Paris-Dakar, the annual all-vehicle rally that goes from Paris south to Dakar, became the official name of this dessert before it even existed. In my mind, the mango represented Dakar and the apple represented Paris, setting a contrasting tone that is both sweet and tart.

1 recipe Pâte Brisée (recipe follows) at room temperature

All-purpose flour, for pan and for dusting

Butter, for pan

FOR THE FILLING

3 eggs

2/3 cup sugar

1 tablespoon grated lemon zest

1/2 cup all-purpose flour

3/4 cup (1 1/2 sticks) unsalted butter

1 vanilla bean, split

2 ripe mangoes, peeled and sliced

2 Granny Smith or Golden Delicious apples, peeled and sliced

FOR THE TOPPING

1 cup sliced Granny Smith apples, sprinkled with lemon juice

2 tablespoons unsalted butter

1/3 cup plus 1 teaspoon sugar

1 cup sliced ripe mango

2 tablespoons apricot jelly

1 tablespoon brandy or water

MAKES ONE 10-INCH TART

1. Preheat the oven to 350°F. With a rolling pin, roll out the pâte brisée on a flour-dusted tabletop to fit a 10-inch tart or pie pan. Butter and flour the inside of the mold before fitting the rolled dough into the pan, trimming the edges. Place in refrigerator while preparing filling.

2. To make the filling: In a bowl, whisk together the eggs, sugar, and zest until combined. Beat in the flour until well mixed.

3. In a small saucepan, heat the butter and vanilla bean over medium heat until brown and foamy. Continue heating until the bubbles subside and the butter is brown and gives off a nutty aroma. Remove the vanilla bean. Whisking continuously, pour the hot butter in a steady stream into the egg mixture, combining well. (The filling can be made ahead up to this point and refrigerated. If so, remove it from the refrigerator and let it come to room temperature before using.)

4. Layer the tart shell with the mango and apple slices. Pour the brown butter mixture over fruit, filling the shell 2/3 full, just above the fruit. To keep the sides of the pastry from falling in during baking, use your finger to seal the dough to the edges of the tart shell with a little bit of brown butter.

5. Bake until nicely browned, 45 to 55 minutes. Let cool completely, at least 2 hours.

6. To make the topping: Meanwhile, sauté the apple in 1 tablespoon butter, 3 to 5 minutes, stirring occasionally. Sprinkle 1 teaspoon of the sugar over the apples and cook at medium heat until thick and caramelized but still firm to the touch. Spread apple slices on a large baking sheet to cool. Repeat with the mango slices, omitting the sugar. When the fruit is cool, decorate the cooled tart, alternating slices of sautéed mango and apple.

7. In a sauté pan set over medium, heat the apricot jelly and remaining 1/3 cup sugar until the jelly liquefies, adding the brandy to help thin the mixture. Using a brush, spread the melted jelly over the fruit slices to give the tart a shiny finish.

Pâte Brisée

1 1/4 cups all-purpose flour

1/4 teaspoon salt

1/2 cup (1 stick) cold unsalted butter, cut into small pieces

1 egg, lightly beaten

1 tablespoon cold water

MAKES ENOUGH FOR
ONE 10-INCH TART

1. Put the flour on a work surface or in a mixing bowl, forming a well in the center. Add the salt and butter to the well. With your fingertips, blend the flour, salt, and butter until you have a crumbly dough. Add the egg, then the water. Knead again with your fingertips until the dough easily forms a ball. Do not overwork the dough. Wrap the dough in plastic wrap. Refrigerate for at least 1 hour.

Madame Mama Diatta Dramé

Madame Safy Gaye

Grilled Pineapple with Ice Cream and Caramel Sauce

1 ripe pineapple, peeled, cored, and sliced into 1/2-inch rounds

Vanilla ice cream

Caramel sauce (recipe follows)

SERVES 6 TO 8

1. Preheat a grill pan or outdoor grill over high heat, or preheat the broiler. Place pineapple slices on grill or under broiler. Cook the slices until brown and nicely caramelized, about 5 minutes. Divide among plates and place a scoop of vanilla ice cream in the center of each, then drizzle with caramel sauce.

Caramel Sauce

Serve this as a syrup over ice cream or over any fruit dessert that meets your fancy. Keep extra caramel sauce refrigerated, and reheat it for future use.

1/2 pound sugar

2 cups heavy cream

MAKES 3 CUPS

1. Cook the sugar over medium heat in a large, heavy saucepan, stirring with a wooden spoon to dissolve all lumps, until it caramelizes, turning deep brown. Use a long-handled spoon to stir in half the heavy cream, being careful to guard against splattering (the mixture will bubble vigorously). When the bubbling subsides, add the rest of the cream and whisk the sauce until it is reduced to the consistency of thick honey.

Millet and Sweet Yogurt (Tiakri)

A favorite restaurant dessert amongst grown-ups, *tiakri* is another after-school snack that Maman would prepare. When sold on street corners, it's poured into clear plastic bags for the kids to slurp on their way home.

2 cups millet couscous (see Glossary)

1/4 cup warm water

Pinch of salt

4 tablespoons (1/2 stick) unsalted butter, at room temperature

4 cinnamon sticks

1/2 cup packed brown sugar

1 teaspoon vanilla extract

1 teaspoon orange flower water (see Glossary)

1 quart Greek yogurt, full fat or lowfat

1 cup confectioners' sugar

1 teaspoon vanilla extract

1/2 teaspoon ground nutmeg

SERVES 6

1. Place the couscous in the top of a steamer lined with cheesecloth. Wet the couscous with 1/4 cup warm water, distributing the water well. Place the steamer top over simmering water, cover, and steam the couscous until tender, about 10 minutes. Add the salt.

2. Remove the couscous to a bowl, fold in the butter, and stir with a spoon or the fingers to evenly coat the couscous.

3. Return the couscous to the steamer with the cinnamon sticks and cook over low heat for 10 more minutes. In a bowl, combine the couscous with the brown sugar, vanilla, and orange water. Stir well.

4. In another bowl, whisk the yogurt with the confectioners' sugar, vanilla, and nutmeg. Place the couscous in bowls and serve with a generous drizzling of the yogurt.

Pineapple Jam

This delicious jam is best served with a buttered toasted baguette. The Senegalese have an obsession with French bread—every street corner has a kiosk or a shop that sells fresh baguettes daily. It's a must to have a baguette in the morning for breakfast in most households. Serve this jam with breakfast or as a sweet ending to a meal.

1 pineapple, peeled and cored

2 cups granulated sugar

Juice of 1 lemon

MAKES ABOUT 2 CUPS

1. In a food processor, coarsely chop the pineapple with sugar and lemon juice. Refrigerate for about 12 hours.

2. Gently boil the pineapple mixture, on medium heat, for 20 to 25 minutes, skimming the foam that rises to the top of the jam. When the jam thickens, transfer it into sterilized half-pint jars and cover tightly. Jam can be refrigerated for up to 4 months.

N'déye Diedhiou from the island of Wendaye

Traditional rof blend

Julie Diatta from Diakene

Green Mango Compote

All over my country, green mango compote is a favorite snack with kids.

6 unripe green mangoes, peeled and cut into chunks

Julienned zest of 1 lime

1 cinnamon stick

1/4 cup sugar, or to taste

SERVES 4

1. Place the mangoes with the lime zest in a pot and add barely enough water to cover the fruit. Add the cinnamon stick and simmer 30 minutes. Remove from heat.

2. Gradually add the sugar, stirring until completely dissolved. Taste for sweetness, adding more sugar as needed. Let sit 1 hour.

3. Return the compote to the stove and cook over medium heat, stirring with a wooden spoon until the liquid is reduced and barely runny, about 10 minutes. Serve warm or chilled.

Chocolate Volcano

This unapologetically chocolaty dessert is a favorite at my restaurant, Le Grand Dakar.

1/2 cup (1 stick) unsalted butter, cut into chunks, plus more for ramekins

Cocoa powder, for dusting

6 ounces bittersweet chocolate, coarsely chopped (or chocolate chips)

2 large eggs plus 2 large egg yolks

3 tablespoons sugar

1/4 cup plus 1 tablespoon sifted all-purpose flour

Vanilla ice cream, for serving

SERVES 6

1. Preheat the oven to 350°F. Grease six 4-ounce ramekins or aluminum foil molds with butter. Dust with cocoa powder and tap out the excess.

2. Over barely simmering water in the top of a double boiler or heatproof bowl, melt the chocolate and 1 stick butter, stirring occasionally until smooth. Remove from heat.

3. In a large bowl, whisk together the eggs, egg yolks, and sugar until well incorporated. Whisk in the melted chocolate and butter. Sift the flour over the top and fold it in.

4. Divide the batter among the ramekins, filling them to 3/4 full. Arrange on a baking dish and bake just until the edges of the cake look set and have pulled slightly away from the sides of the ramekins, 5 to 6 minutes. The centers should remain slightly liquid; do not over bake.

5. Turn the volcanoes out onto a plate and serve immediately with vanilla ice cream.

Banana Fritters

1 1/2 cups all-purpose flour

6 tablespoons sugar

3 eggs

1 cup milk

4 or 5 ripe bananas (about 1 pound)

Vegetable oil, for deep-frying

Confectioners' sugar

MAKES ABOUT 20 FRITTERS

1. In a large bowl, stir the flour and sugar together. With an electric mixer, beat in the eggs one at a time. Slowly add the milk and mix until the batter is smooth and stretches like a ribbon.

2. Coarsely chop the bananas and place them in a bowl. With a fork, mash the bananas into a smooth puree. Stir the puree into the batter and let the mixture rest for at least 30 minutes before frying.

3. Pour the oil into a deep saucepan to a depth of 2 to 3 inches and heat to 365°F. Drop 2 tablespoons banana batter into the hot oil, deep-frying 2 or 3 fritters at a time, leaving enough space so they can spread. Fry for about 3 minutes or until the fritters are golden brown, turning once with a slotted spoon. Drain on paper towels. Sprinkle with confectioners' sugar and serve warm.

Carrot, Coconut, and Pineapple Cake

1 1/2 cups peanut or canola oil, plus more for pan

1 1/2 cups all-purpose flour, plus more for pan

1 1/2 cups sugar

5 large eggs

2 teaspoons ground cinnamon

1 teaspoon nutmeg

1 teaspoon baking soda

1 teaspoon baking powder

2 teaspoons vanilla extract

3 cups grated carrot

1 cup shredded unsweetened coconut

1 cup drained crushed pineapple

1/2 cup chopped walnuts (optional)

MAKES ONE 14 X 8-INCH CAKE

1. Preheat oven to 350°F. Oil a 14 x 8-inch baking pan and dust with flour. Mix the sugar and eggs with an electric mixer at high speed until fluffy and pale. Slowly pour the oil into the egg mixture while mixing.

2. In a large bowl, sift together the flour, cinnamon, nutmeg, baking soda, and baking powder. Pour the dry ingredients into the egg mixture and continue to mix. Add the vanilla and remaining ingredients. Stop mixing when all ingredients are combined.

3. Pour the batter into the prepared pan and bake until a toothpick inserted in the middle comes out dry, 45 to 50 minutes. If desired, dust with confectioners' sugar and serve with ice cream.

DRINKS

Sorrel (Bissap)

Sorrel is an herb in the buckwheat family. Its flowers—usually red, sometimes yellow—are dried and infused in hot water. Chilled, sweetened, and combined with lime or pineapple juice, it can be quite refreshing. It's a popular drink throughout West Africa, and chances are you will be offered a glass of it when visiting a Senegalese household. It has medicinal uses as well; in Senegal it is sometimes mixed with other roots to cure the flu or extreme fatigue. As with many other culinary traditions, sorrel juice traveled to the Caribbean by way of the Middle Passage.

1/4 pound dried sorrel flower

2 cups water

1/4 cup mint leaves

1/2 cup honey

1 quart water

SERVES 10

1. Wash the sorrel under cold running water. In a saucepan, bring 2 cups water to a boil. Reduce heat, add sorrel flower and mint and simmer about 5 minutes.

2. Off the heat, sweeten with the honey and add 1 quart water. Strain and refrigerate. Serve cold.

Ginger Beer

Ginger beer is another Senegalese favorite that survived the hardships of the African odyssey to become a popular drink in the Caribbean. There, the roots are boiled in water, whereas in Senegal, we crush the ginger in a mortar and pestle with a little water. This concentrated ginger is then strained, diluted with more water, and sweetened. We also use it in traditional medicine as a cure for arthritis.

l/2 pound ginger root

4 cups water

4 limes

1/2 cup honey or sugar

SERVES 10

1. Rinse ginger roots thoroughly in running water. Peel and roughly chop them.

2. In a blender, combine ginger with 1 cup water, and process until liquefied. Strain well and add the remaining 3 cups water, the lime juice, and honey. Taste and adjust with more water and honey if the drink is too strong for your liking. Serve cold.

Attaya

In Senegal and throughout West Africa, life is cadenced by the ritual of the tea ceremony. *Attaya* can be served at any moment. While the tea is being prepared, friends and family sit around on straw mats or on low benches, have conversations, tell jokes, or simply relax. *Les Trois Normaux*, as it is also called, is served in three symbolic stages. The first tea is bitter, like life; the second is sweet, like love; and the third is gentle, like the breath of death. *Attaya* is always served with foam topping the tiny tea glasses *(kas)*. This foam results from pouring attaya from one kas to another, slowly, in a long stream from as high as the tea maker's expertise allows, without spilling (this takes practice). This process is repeated back and forth until each *kas* has accumulated a nice amount of foam.

3 cups water

5 tablespoons Chinese green tea (Gunpowder brand)

1 cup sugar

1 small bunch mint leaves

SERVES 4

EQUIPMENT

1 *barada:* small teapot

4 *kas:* tiny tea glasses

Round 1 *(Lewel)*

In a small teapot *(barada)* put 1 cup water and 4 tablespoons tea leaves *(warga)*. Set the pot over medium heat and bring the mix to a boil. Remove from heat and pour some of the tea into each of the 4 small glasses. Begin pouring the liquid back and forth between the glasses until each glass has foam in it. Keeping the foam in the glasses, pour the liquid back into the *barada*, add about 1/4 cup sugar and bring to a simmer. Remove from heat and pour the tea into the glasses. Pour back and forth until there is more foam, then serve.

Round 2 *(Niarel)*

Add 1 cup water to the teapot (tea leaves should still be in the pot). Add 2 sprigs of mint leaves *(nana)*. Bring to a boil. Add 1/4 cup sugar; bring to a boil again. Remove from heat and pour tea into each of the same glasses. Begin pouring the liquid back and forth between the glasses until each one has foam in it. Keeping the foam in the glasses, pour the liquid back into the brada and bring to a boil. Remove from heat and pour into the glasses. Continue pouring from glass to glass until there is more foam, then serve.

Round 3 *(Nietel)*

Add 1 cup water and 1 tablespoon tea leaves to the pot, keeping the leaves and mint from the previous rounds in the pot. Add the remaining mint leaves (be generous as this part must be sweeter). Bring to a boil. Add 1/2 cup sugar and bring to a boil. Remove from heat and pour some of the tea into each glass. Pour the liquid back and forth between the glasses until each glass has foam in it. Keeping the foam in the glasses, pour the liquid back into the *brada* and bring to a boil again. Remove from heat and pour into the glasses. Mix again until there is even more foam, then serve round 3.

Abdou N'daw preparing attaya

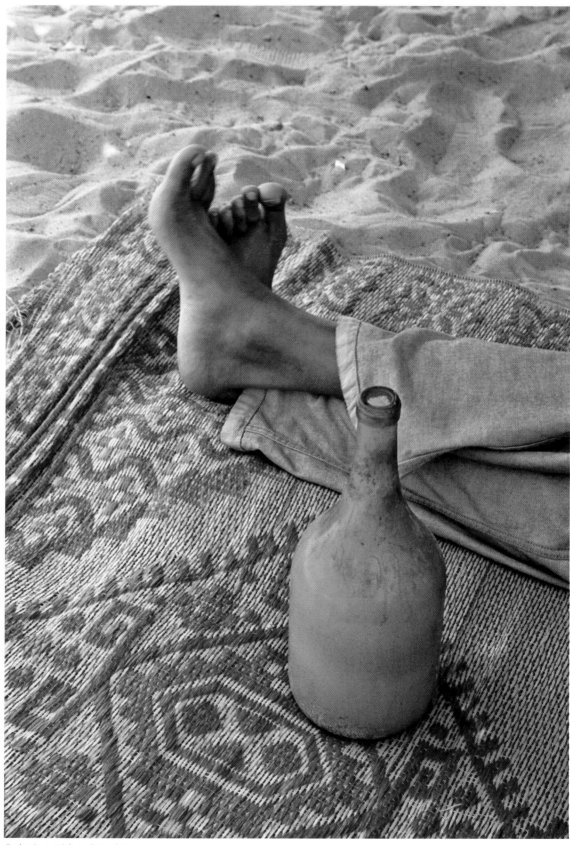

Relaxing with palm wine

Bouye

Bouye is the fruit of the baobab tree. It is also called *pain de singe* ("monkey's bread") in French. Besides making a delicious drink, it is used in cooking and to cure many ills, including fatigue.

1/2 pound *bouye* (see Glossary)

2 quarts water

1/2 cup sugar

1 teaspoon orange flower water (see Glossary)

SERVES 8 TO 10

1. Soak baobab fruit in 2 quarts water, about 15 minutes.

2. Using your hands, extract the pulp from the seeds, and strain. Discard the seeds and fibers.

3. Add the sugar and orange flower water to the liquid; stir to combine. Serve cold.

Tamarind Juice (Dakhar)

The tamarind fruit comes from a thorny tree, *tamarinier*, that grows abundantly in our region. Dakar, our capital city, is named after this fruit. Legend has it that the French colonizers were unable to pronounce the Wolof "kh" sound of Dakhar, in which the "k" is aspirated. Sweet and sour, the tamarind comes in a pod. It can be cracked and eaten as is, or diluted with water, sweetened, and strained to make this drink.

1/4 pound tamarind paste (see Glossary)

4 cups tepid water

1 cup sugar

SERVES 10

1. Soak tamarind in 1 cup water, about 30 minutes.

2. With your bare hands or a spoon, extract tamarind juice by squeezing paste. Strain tamarind, reserving juice, and repeat process in remaining water.

3. Sweeten the juice with the sugar and refrigerate. Serve cold.

PARTY MENUS

New Year's Day Menu

Black-Eyed Pea Fritters
Bakary Calamari Salad
Cornish Hen Farci au Fonio
Chocolate Volcano

Summer Menus

Green Plantain Chips
Avocado-Mango Salad
Rack of Venison Baked in Kraft Paper
    (Dibi Biche)
Grilled Pineapple with Caramel Sauce

Yuca Couscous Salad (Athieke Salad)
Blue Fish with Red Rice and Vegetables
    (Thiebou Jen)
Green Mango Compote
Sorrel (Bissap)

Black-Eyed Pea Salad (Salatu Niebe)
Grilled Chicken with Lime-Onion Sauce
    (Yassa Ginaar)
Grilled Sweet Potatoes
Banana Fritters

Fall Menus

Fried Sweet Plantains (Aloco)
Fried Fish and Ragout (Thiou)
Millet and Sweet Yogurt (Tiakri)
Tamarind Juice (Dakhar)

Fish Croquettes (Boulettes)
Soupi Kandja Royale
Senegalese Mint Tea (Attaya)
Chocolate Volcano

Winter Menus

Beef Knuckle Soup (Soupou Yell)
Crab St. Louis-Style (Cotis Ndar)
Steamed Fonio and Crushed Peanuts with
    Spicy Eggplant (Djouka de Fonio)
Chocolate Volcano

Millet Beef Croquettes
Five-Spice Duck
West African Yam Paste Balls (Fufu)
Roasted Mango and Coconut Rice Pudding
    (Sombi)

Shrimp and Sweet Potato Fritters
Steamed Millet with Poached Tilapia
    (Muuda Joola)
Paris-Dakar: Apple-Mango Tart
Ginger Beer

Spring Menus

Green Mango Salad (Niambaan)
Fonio Taboule
Paris-Dakar: Apple-Mango Tart

Vegetarian Spring Rolls
Oyster Elinkine
Grouper and Millet "Polenta" (Niiri Liidi)
Carrot, Coconut, and Pineapple Cake

Shrimp and Melon Salad
Lamb and Vegetable Stew with Millet
    Couscous (Thiere Neverdaye)
Green Mango Compote

GLOSSARY

Athieke: Fine grainy meal, similar in consistency to flour. prepared from the dried pulp of the yuca. Available in West African food stores.

Bouye: Fruit of the Baobab tree with a unique pleasant flavor and a mild slightly acidic aftertaste. Bouye is very rich in vitamin C and iron. Available in some specialty stores.

Diaxatou: Bitter eggplant with a distinct taste. This African eggplant is used in traditional Senegalese dishes and is said to have some medicinal uses. Regular eggplants can be substituted. Look for *diaxatou* in some Mexican food stores.

Dried Clams: Clams that have been removed from their shells and dried in the sun. Available in Asian food stores.

Dried Oysters: These are oysters which have been shelled and dried in the sun. Available in Asian food stores.

Dried Shrimp: Sold in Asian or Latin American groceries and markets, these whole tiny dried shrimp may be pulverized at home in a blender. Store in refrigerator. Be sure to wash dried shrimp before using.

Fish Sauce: Also known as *nuoc mam*, fish sauce is made from anchovies or other small fish, fermented with salt, and stored in barrels for a lengthy period (6 months to sometimes years). Fish sauce is a good substitute for *guedj* and *yet*. Available in Southeast Asian stores and supermarkets.

Fonio: Fonio *(Digitaria exilis)* has been grown in West Africa for centuries. For a long time, it was of marginal importance as a cereal due to its small seeds, but is now the object of renewed interest as consumers begin to recognize its flavor and nutritional qualities.

Fonio is one of the most nutritious of all grains. It is rich in methionine and cystine, amino acids vital to human health and deficient in today's major cereals: wheat, rice, maize, sorghum, barley, and rye. This combination of nutrition and taste could be of outstanding future importance. Fonio can found in some specialty stores or online sources.

Ground Peanut Flour: Peanuts pounded or processed to the point of pulverisation.

Guedj: Dried fermented fish, with a pungent, salty flavor. Used whole or crumbled as a seasoning in stews and sauces.

Kong: Senegalese smoked catfish. The flavor can be similar to the smoked chicken or smoked turkey legs found in Latin American food markets.

Millet Couscous: Millet is highly nutritious, non-glutinous grain. It is tasty, with a mildly sweet, nutty flavor and contains a myriad of beneficial nutrients. It is nearly 15% protein, contains high amounts of fiber, B-complex vitamins, the essential amino acid methionine, lecithin, and some vitamin E. It is particularly high in iron, magnesium, phosphorous, and potassium. Look for millet couscous in some specialty stores.

Orange Flower Water: Flavoring made from the distillation of fresh orange blossoms. It's mostly used in Middle Eastern cuisine. Available year round in Middle Eastern food stores.

Palm oil: Americans often assume that consuming palm oil is unhealthy. However, it is important to distinguish between palm oil and palm kernel oil or coconut oil—palm oil from the fruit of the palm is physically and chemically different from both the palm kernel oil (extracted from the fruit seeds), and from coconut oil, both of which are highly saturated. Palm oil itself is reddish because it contains a high amount of beta carotene rich in vitamin A and antioxidants. Palm oil is free of cholesterol and trans fats. Palm oil is said to be nature's gift to the world—its nutritional value, health benefits, and value as a natural resource continue to be explored even today. It can be found in Brazilian stores as "dende oil."

Preserved lemons: Lemons preserved in salt brine for up to two months. The softened rind is chopped and added at the last stage of cooking. Available in Middle Eastern stores.

Ras el hanout: Moroccan blend of spices comprising up to fifty ingredients, including ground ginger, anise, cinnamon, nutmeg, dried rose petal, and turmeric. Available year round in Middle Eastern food stores.

Shrimp paste: Shrimp paste is a common ingredient used in Southeast Asian cuisine. It is made from fermented ground shrimp and has a very strong odor. It can be found in Asian markets.

Tamarind: Tree that grows in Africa, Southeast Asia, Latin America, and India. The fruit comes in pods and is sharp and sour in taste. The pulp can be bought compressed or in paste form. The former must be boiled in water and strained to discard the fibers and seeds. Available in Latin American or Asian stores.

Yet: A marine snail also known as conch, *yet* is made by drying these mollusks in the sunlight for a lengthy period of time until it ferments. It has a strong odor and is used in stews and sauces. It is found in Senegalese markets and can be substituted with fish sauce.

Yuca: A long starchy root vegetable with rough brown bark-like skin and a hard white interior. Available year-round in Latin American markets.

Mail order source for bouye, guedj, millet couscous, fonio, and yet:

GIE Maria Distribution
Sicap Sacre-Coeur 3, Villa 8851,
Rue Oumar Pene
Dakar, Senegal
Tel 221 33 827 3975

AUTHOR'S NOTE

At first New York was just a short stop on my way to Cleveland, Ohio. I was headed for Baldwin Wallace College, a school to which I had applied while still in Senegal, to finish my physics and chemistry degree. I had planned this trip with my friend Habib, whom I somehow had convinced to come with me rather than go to a school in Belgium.

We really just wanted to explore the world; Dakar had become boring to us. Our university, Cheikh Anta Diop, once a cradle of knowledge where many of the African elite had studied, was closed. The late eighties were marred with student strikes. For the first time, the government decided to declare an *Année Blanche* (Blank Year). Many of us just couldn't accept the idea of a whole school year lost. I was raised in a family that praised school diplomas. The timing was perfect to convince my parents. We just had to go.

Habib arrived a few months before me and went straight to Cleveland. His mission was to organize our lodging and scout for jobs, because we barely had enough money for our tuition. Meanwhile, I had planned to stay in New York for a couple of weeks. I could stay with Vieux, a friend from Senegal who was sharing a room with three other roommates. The "room" in question was at the end of a narrow hallway full of graffiti and reeking of foul odors. It was in a dingy building on 50th Street, called Hotel Cinquante, near Times Square. Most of the tenants were *modou-modou*,[1] drug dealers, or prostitutes.

Two beds occupied most of the space in our room, except for a narrow area where someone had placed a cheap commode for his *attaya* (see recipe page 156) set. Across the room sat a dresser, atop which dusty suitcases were piled. Five of us shared the room, not counting, of course, the rats that would go about their business as soon as the lights were turned off. Ras, another roommate, tried to reassure me that they were inoffensive and that anyway, Hotel Cinquante really belonged to the rats and we should be thankful that they were accommodating us! In this lovely setting, three days after I arrived,

1. This is what we Dakarois call the immigrants from the countryside. They are easily spotted on streets and avenues of every big city in the world (Paris, Rome, Hong-Kong, New York, etc.). The tall, dark, slim man selling fake Rolex watches, Louis Vuitton bags, or umbrellas (when it rains)—that's a *modou*. He usually hails from the Baol region of Senegal, is a big traveler, and is more than likely a Mouride. Mouridism is a major spiritual movement in Senegal. Disciples of Cheikh Ahmadou Bamba, its adherents are Sufi Muslims, who practice a tradition of self-reliance. A strong work ethic and an entrepreneurial spirit are characteristics of the Mourides. They built Touba, their holy land, from a little village into the second largest city in Senegal.

all my money was stolen from my suitcase.

I had just lost my father's hard-earned money. I didn't even have the bus fare to Cleveland; I was stuck in New York. Returning back home was certainly not an option. In fact, to this day, I have never told my Dad what happened.

Luckily, Samba, another of my roommates, knew of a job opening at a restaurant where he was a dishwasher. Out of options, I was hired as a busboy at Garvin's, an American restaurant in the West Village. Anytime I got a chance, I would sneak into the kitchen to chat in Wolof with Samba. I was intrigued by the men in white moving in harmony around the flames and knives. It was theatrical, almost magical. A waiter would bring in a ticket and someone would read it aloud; within minutes, a tray full of delicious dishes would leave the kitchen.

Men cooking! The kitchen felt like a world apart. These men in white were sharing a secret; it seemed as if they must have gone through a rite of passage, an initiation to awaken some buried feminine intuition that makes one a good cook. As far as I knew only women could excel in cooking. I was drawn into this universe of pots and pans.

I couldn't stay too much longer without giving a report on my situation to my parents. I had been here for one month already, and time was passing. Without any realistic way to go to college this year, I had to come up with a plan B. Cooking! The choice felt right, regardless of the cultural restraints in my country. The kitchen was not a place for men I had always been told.

But how to tell my parents? I didn't think they were ready to hear that I'd changed (or should I say lost?) my mind and decided to become a cook. Nor that I'd lost all their money! They would have thought that I'd gone mad and would die worrying about me on my own in New York. A young man telling his parents he was going to be a cook was like telling them he was running off to join the circus. It just wasn't something like being an engineer, a doctor, or a lawyer. To muster the courage, I told my friends first, and then my siblings. I still remember how hard my cousin Alice laughed when she heard that I was cooking. Maybe unconsciously I knew that I'd never have to tell my parents by using this strategy, because they found out, anyway, through the grapevine. The real surprise came in their reaction. They were open-minded about it, and my mother, perhaps because of her keen passion for cooking, was even encouraging. My father, too, surprised me by not challenging my unusual career choice.

I may not have had any money, but I could still get educated.
I located a library near the East Village and went straight to the cooking section. That became my new sanctuary. Every day I would find a couple of hours to spend there, reading Julia Child, taking notes on classic French recipes, and experimenting in the kitchen. It seemed like a déjà vu from my childhood days when I would sit on a chair near the bookshelf where Maman kept her *Larousse Gastronomique* collection.

Habib would sometimes visit during school breaks. He couldn't believe how focused I was on my Julia Child books. He hadn't seen me studying that intensely since the time we were preparing for our baccalaureates. Back then we would stay up all night studying and drinking *attaya* to stay awake. Since kindergarten, our parents had inculcated in us the importance of education; getting our diploma seemed to be the only key to a decent future. In my new life, the key to that door was cooking.

Cliff, a waiter at Garvin's, told me of a new restaurant opening in the West Village. I decided to apply for a job there, not as a busboy, but as a cook. The interview went well, partly, I suspect, because I lied, saying that I had just arrived from France, where I had been living. That chef loved everything French. My name being Pierre and my "Parisian" accent, mastered while a teenager in the Dakar eighties, helped quite a bit, I must confess.

I started as a Garde-Manger. The salad station, as it is also called, was mainly about making dressings, prepping and assembling salads. The concept of a salad dressing, for example, creating an emulsion of an acid liquid (vinegar or citrus) and a lipid (oil), was familiar to me considering my background in chemistry. Understanding the interaction of ingredients was one of the great advantages my school years provided to my new career. The kitchen was really just a chemistry lab, but one that frankly seemed much more fun. Habib, now a chemical engineer, also agrees. Over time, my skills were recognized and I was given more and more responsibilities in the kitchen.

My first day at the grill station started as a nightmare. Jaime, a quick-tempered Ecuadorian cook didn't show up for his shift one busy night. I was asked to step up. My head was pounding and my chef coat drenched with sweat from the heat of the burning grill. Had I listened to a persistent voice in my head, I would have simply walked away. It was telling me to undo my apron, unbutton my white jacket, slip into regular clothes, and walk far away from this grill, this restaurant, without ever looking back. My years in the chemistry lab hadn't prepared me for this one.

I cleaned myself up and resolutely returned to the grill; I couldn't give up. The pounding headache, the burning heat from the grill—nothing would deter me from pursuing my new dream. That day was a turning point. Later that night, while celebrating with the rest of the kitchen team what had been a record night, I was officially declared the new grill person. How I manned the grill that night had impressed the chef.

My motivation quadrupled. My only activities for the following ten years were spent between the kitchen and the cookbooks at the library. I wanted to become an accomplished chef. The French cooking classics became my favorite readings. Again, my physics and chemistry background came in handy. After all, the methods and principles of cooking are nothing but physical phenomena. Transforming ingredients with heat transmitted though conduction (direct fire, oven, or hot liquid), or cold cooking them with citric acid (lemon juice in a ceviche) were techniques that I could easily grasp.

It wasn't until many years later, after I had paid my dues in different kitchens around the city, that I started to look back at the food I grew up eating. My parents had accepted my new life more easily than I had expected. Maman, who was as passionate as I was about food, started sharing her secret recipes with me. Every time I would visit home, I would spend more time with Maman or my aunts in the kitchen, learning the tricks of our grandmothers' trade. I would come back to New York, eager to cook Senegalese food for my colleagues. I was working in a tiny French Bistro on Sullivan Street in Soho, *Jean-Claude*, when I heard of a new restaurant on Spring Street, a couple of blocks away. The cuisine at *Boom* dubbed "global ethnic" was receiving great reviews. The chef and owner, Geoffray Murray, a tall man with long blond hair, looked more like a surfer than a chef. He had traveled the world and it reflected on his food. His flavors were bold and authentic, the inspiration being Southeast Asian with some North African influences.

After working at *Boom* for a few years, I was offered a sous-chef position, replacing Vinny, a Sicilian chef who was promoted to open a new sister restaurant in South Beach, Miami. Soon, I was being asked for recipes from my country with any menu revision. The reception was fantastic. Geoffray helped me rediscover my own Senegalese cuisine.

Boom and Soho became trendy. Geoffray and I, now best friends, deplored the changes. An opportunity came to open *Two Rooms* uptown. The concept was great. Geoffray would present fine classics in an intimate dining room downstairs while I would offer less formal African-inspired fare in the Karoo room upstairs. *Two Rooms* soon became a hit. Sadly, our young Wall Street investors wanted to recreate trendy Soho in our uptown space. Geoffray, sensing the danger, accepted a position as executive chef of an exclusive South African resort, and was gone.

Meanwhile, I had married and my wife Umaimah and I were expecting Sitoë, our daughter. I would never return to the wild party days of Soho. In the summer of 1997, on Independence Day precisely, I started Sage, a catering company with a mission to offer the curious and informed, upscale, festive Senegalese food and beyond. My friend Barry Friedberg became my partner. Ten years later the adventure continues with *Le Grand Dakar*, where music, art, and even literature complement my concept of introducing African food to our guests.

ACKNOWLEDGMENTS

These pages would have never been written if it weren't for the enormous contributions I've received along the way. My thanks go to all the following:

Tata Marie Mathiam and Mamma Douba Kande, you channeled Maman's spirit, tirelessly and graciously revisiting traditional recipes for the sake of this project.

Henriette Vieyra-Sambou and the lovely food that always comes out of your kitchen.

Marthe Nunez-Coly for your succulent gumbo.

My Publisher and the Lake Isle Press team, Hiroko Kiiffner, Kate Trimble, and Pimpila Thanaporn. Your vision, patience and meticulous guidance were key ingredients in making this happen.

Adam Bartos, who first had the idea, and whose photographs complement the recipes. I am grateful for your friendship. Your sensibility is felt through these remarkable depictions of my culture.

Carol Amoruso for your immense contribution in the writing process, this book is as much yours as mine.

Carole Lalli for unselfishly donating your experience and time.

David and Joanna Novros, for sharing the same passion—good food without borders—and for meticulously reading and correcting these pages.

Gary Sofizade, Ely Kane, and Habib Diallo, your enthusiasm and support kept me going.

The Sall family and their restaurant Keur Ndeye in Dakar that still serves the best thiebou jen in town.

Djibril Diallo at the UNPD, I can't thank you enough for your enthusiasm and faith in this book.

To Moko, for you are always present—a true friend and supporter.

To my friend and elder Randy Weston for keeping me rooted through his unwavering commitment to Africa.

To Nach Waxman and the Kitchen Arts and Letters team for your encouragement.

To Mme Bintou Ndiaye and Mr. Aziz Gueye at the Senegalese Tourism Bureau in New York for your support and your friendship.

To Madame Fall (Ameth's mom) for the best Tamkharit memories with your succulent couscous.

To Hugues Segla for sharing your mom's secret recipes.

To chefs Bocar Mamadou Diallo, Gaby Gueye, and David Diatta of the "Association des Chefs de Cuisine du Senegal" for their commitment to Senegalese cuisine.

To my friends in Senegal who showed to me the real meaning of teranga during my many trips while working on this book: Didier and Jeanine Diop, Pape Diagne, Benoit Sambou, Jean-Michel Mathiam, Alexandre Thiam, and the women in the villages of Diakene Diola and Elinkine who generously offered their time and shared their recipes.

Last but not least to my wife, Umaimah, and my children, Sitoë, Elijah, and Haroun. I love you.

INDEX

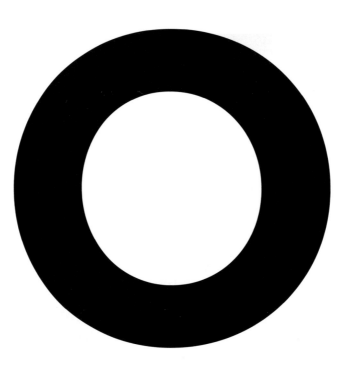

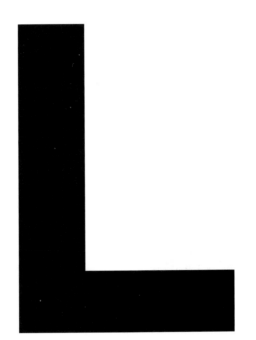

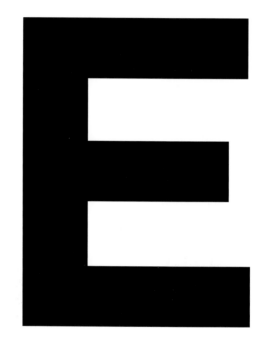

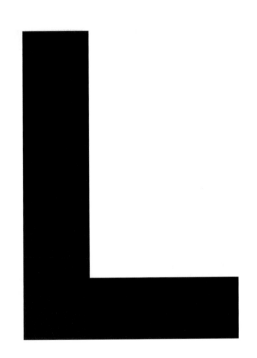

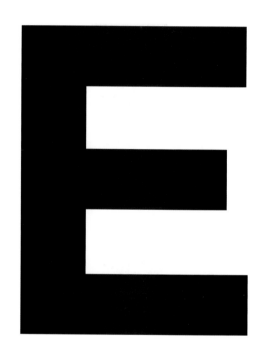

Pierre Thiam was born in Dakar, Senegal. He was raised in this most cosmopolitan of African cities and in Senegal's southernmost coastal province, Casamance. In Dakar, he enjoyed Senegalese, French, Vietnamese, and Moroccan cuisines routinely, while in Casamance he was treated to age-old indigenous flavors and foods influenced by Portuguese colonists.

Pierre came to the States in the late 80s and devoted himself to exploring the city's many ethnic cuisines. He went from garde-manger to chef de cuisine at *Jean-Claude* and *Boom* in Soho, and on to *Bang*, in South Beach, Miami. He designed innovative, eclectic African menus at *Zanzibar* and *Two Rooms* on the Upper East Side, and launched two kosher restaurants in Brooklyn, one serving Vietnamese fare.

Presently, Pierre is the chef and owner of *Le Grand-Dakar* (opened in 2004) in Clinton Hill, Brooklyn, which specializes in West African cuisine, and has become a home-away-from-home to many African artists and musicians.

Adam Bartos's work is included in the permanent collections of the Museum of Modern Art, New York; the San Francisco Museum of Modern Art; the J. Paul Getty Museum, Los Angeles; and others. Bartos is noted for his books *International Territory: The United Nations 1945-1995* (Verso, 1994), *Kosmos: A Portrait of the Russian Space Age* (Princeton Architectural Press, 2001), and *Boulevard* (Steidl/Dangin 2006). His next monograph, *Yard Sale Photographs*, will be published in Spring 2009.

DISCARD